The Architecture of Europe

The Ancient Classical and Byzantine World, 3000 B.C.–A.D. 1453

Also by Doreen Yarwood

Published

English Costume
The English Home
The Architecture of England
The Outline of English Architecture
English Houses
The Outline of English Costume
The Architecture of Italy
Robert Adam
The Architecture of Europe
European Costume
The Architecture of Britain
Encyclopedia of World Costume
Costume of the Western World
The British Kitchen
Five Hundred Years of Technology in the Home
English Interiors
Encyclopedia of Architecture
Chronology of Western Architecture
Fashion in the Western World
The Architecture of Europe
Volume 1 The Ancient Classical and Byzantine
    World 3000 BC–AD 1453
Volume 2 The Middle Ages 650–1550
Volume 3 Classical Architecture 1420–1800
Volume 4 The 19th and 20th Centuries

The Architecture of Europe

The Ancient Classical and Byzantine World
3000 B.C.–A.D. 1453

Doreen Yarwood

Volume 1

B.T. Batsford Ltd, London

Doreen Yarwood 1992
First published 1992

Typeset by
Servis Filmsetting Ltd, Longsight, Manchester
and printed in Great Britain
by Courier International Ltd
East Kilbride, Scotland
for the publishers
B.T. Batsford Ltd
4 Fitzhardinge Street
London W1H 0AH

A CIP catalogue for this book is
available from the British Library

ISBN 0 7134 6962 5

Contents

4 Civic Planning and the Grid Town Layout

Preface

There are many books available on the architecture of Europe. Most of these cover a specific area or period and a number present the subject in a general way. It is rare for one in the English language to deal with Europe as a whole; generally only western Europe is discussed and, within this context, a careful selection of western European countries. This is understandable, especially in the light of the older, academic approach to the subject, for it was long considered that only countries such as France, Italy and possibly Germany and the Low Countries had been instrumental in influencing and forming British architectural history.

Since 1945, with increasing leisure time, the expansion of higher education and, above all, a greater facility of travel, the whole of Europe has become opened up to tourists and students and academic study has broadened its base. It has gradually become easier to visit Eastern Europe and the U.S.S.R.

In 1963 the publishers and I decided that I should write and illustrate a book which would narrate simply and chronologically the history of European architecture showing the building development and interdependence of the 23 countries concerned from the time of Ancient Greece to the present day.

The book, which was published in 1974, occupied 10 years of my time and our travels were carried out during my husband's college vacations. The area covered was confined to the geographical limits of Europe. It has been very successful, being reprinted several times but now, with the widening of scope and greater ease of travel, far more people are able and interested to visit areas further afield. It was felt that, for the classical remains discussed in this volume, that Asia Minor, though not part of Europe, should be included. For this reason a supplementary chapter has been added at the end of this book which discusses and illustrates not only the remains in Turkey but further relevant information, updating and coverage upon the volume as a whole.

This is an immense canvas even for a work of this size and there can be no pretence of comprehensiveness or detail. The aim is to present as clear a picture as possible of the general evolution of style and taste in different areas, illustrating which trends, political, social, climatic, etc., influenced certain areas at certain times. I have given greater space in each chapter to the countries which were of paramount importance in leading certain movements and which produced the finest work of that age. The areas concerned vary from century to century: Greece and Rome in the classical world, France in the Middle Ages, Italy in the Renaissance, Germany and Finland in the twentieth century. I have also given especial coverage to countries in eastern and northern Europe which tend to have been left out of books on European architecture. In this volume the development of classical architecture is traced from its early beginnings in the Minoan and Mycenaean cultures to the supreme achievement of classical Greece and on to its extension into Hellenistic, Etruscan and Roman forms. The continuance of the Roman Empire in its eastern part, centred on Constantinople, is then discussed together with the emergence of an early Christian form of architecture and the later Byzantine work strongly influenced by eastern design.

Half the space is devoted to illustration, for architecture is a visual object. My husband, John Yarwood, and I have travelled some 67,000 miles in Europe, mainly by car, visiting each of the countries, many of them several times. My husband has taken over 25,000 photographs from which the illustrations, both line drawings and photographic plates, have been made.

In Europe, as on a small scale in England, great buildings are constantly in process of demolition and alteration. Even today few of the books available on European architecture provide a reliable guide to the present state of such monuments. I hope that at least for a few years, this book will provide an up-to-date guide on the condition and existence of interesting architectural work. In our travels we have encountered many discrepancies from written descriptions; some buildings referred to as intact were totally destroyed in the Second World War, others have been demolished, adapted, restored or altered. This is a continuous process and only constant study can present an accurate overall picture.

I hope that one of the uses of this book may be to encourage readers to go to see buildings *in situ*. With this in mind, I have not followed the common tradition of naming buildings and places according to the time of their construction, but have referred to them by the names used currently in their present countries, names to be found readily in standard atlases and guide books.

I should like to express my appreciation to colleagues and friends who have provided me with data and photographs for areas which I was not able to visit. I should like to thank especially Miss Margaret Briggs for her work at Knossos and Mr. Vjachaslav Orelski and his colleagues from the Union of Architects in Moscow who assisted me greatly in that city and provided me with material on the more remote cities in the northern European areas of the USSR which lack of time made it impossible for me to visit. Most of all I wish to express my appreciation to my husband, Professor John Yarwood, not only for accompanying me on all the travels and taking the photographs, but for developing and printing them which was much more of a chore.

The author and publishers wish to thank the British Museum for permission to reproduce plates 2, 4, 5, 7 and 18, and Mr. A.F. Kersting A.I.I.P., F.R.P.S., for plate 36. The remainder of the photographic plates were taken by my husband, Professor John Yarwood, and myself.

East Grinstead 1991   *Doreen Yarwood*

Minoan and Greek: *c.* 3000–146 B.C.

Pre-Hellenic Greece: The Bronze Age *c.* 3000–1100 B.C.

Remains survive of Neolithic and Early Bronze Age building by the peoples inhabiting islands and mainland areas in the Aegean dating from about 3000 B.C., but these early constructions are not architecture and only provide architectural interest because of the influence which they exerted on later peoples. Greece is poor in material resources and timber for building has always been scarce and difficult to transport across mountain regions. The chief material, therefore, in those times was sun-dried brick, made in summer sunshine, and built upon a base of stone blocks with a floor of beaten earth. Even from early times these Mediterranean peoples used the trabeated constructional form of posts or

walls and horizontal lintels to support roofs or make openings.

The *chief centres of civilisation* in Bronze Age Greece were on the coast of Asia Minor, the islands, particularly Crete, and the later mainland developments of Mycenae. Building work of this culture is commonly divided into three parts: early, *c.* 3000–2000 B.C., middle, *c.* 2000–1600 B.C., and late, *c.* 1600–1100 B.C. The work is called by different names according to definition: Pelasgic after the race of people, Minoan after King Minos of Crete, Aegean after the area of occupation or Mycenaean after the later settlements. Archaeological study is still yielding new information, particularly in more accurate dating of the work; the whole subject of this period of development is comparatively recent in discovery, dating only from the original, magnificent achievements of Heinrich Schliemann at Mycenae and Tiryns and Sir Arthur Evans at Knossos in the late nineteenth century and early twentieth. The early peoples were intent on providing shelter and protection for themselves and, therefore, remains from the first period came from houses and fortifications. Later ages yield palaces, tombs and more elaborate walled towns with fortified gates. Types of walling are large scale in rough cyclopean blocks with small stones and clay in the interstices or later polygonal courses, while designs of columns, fresco decoration, jewellery and arms show influence of Egyptian and Assyrian culture, although unmistakably Minoan or Mycenaean. The later Hellenic peoples of Greece also borrowed much from their Bronze Age ancestors, particularly in ornamental forms. Columns characteristically taper inwards towards the base (there are two of these standing outside the museum at Eleusis (**20**), and there are also those from the Treasury of Atreus now in the British Museum (**59**). Roofs are often vaulted in triangular or barrel vault form. Stone blocks in horizontal courses are built to project inwards one above the other to form the vault. There is a fine triangular example at Tiryns (**9**) and the bee-hive tombs at Mycenae are dome-shaped. Openings from the earlier times are triangular headed with large blocks forming the openings (**6** and **11**) while later examples have horizontal lintel stones (**5** and **10**).

Minoan Architecture in Crete

Here there were a number of building periods, of which two produced a high standard of work: the first climax came in the middle Minoan period from *c.* 2000 to 1600 B.C. and the second in the late Minoan period up to 1100 B.C. In the first of these were built the palaces at *Knossos, Phaistos* and *Mallia.* This is presumed to be the era of King Minos, whose name has come down to us in Greek legends, and it is also the time of active foreign trading and a flourishing activity in building and the arts. The second climax brought larger palaces, wealth for the upper classes and spacious architecture which boasted adequate sanitation systems. Walls and ceilings were decorated with brilliantly coloured fresco paintings in their now characteristic ornamental forms of continuous scrolls (**64**), fret and guilloche and of lively human and animal forms, the former in vividly depicted dress. Examples, partly restored, can be seen in the National Museum in Athens. Here also discoveries were made in gold, silver, ivory, faïence and terracotta of sculpture and ornament from the tombs showing the characteristic Minoan forms which, like the architecture, owed something to Egypt but lacked its monumentality. The palace architecture of the best Cretan work illustrates an adaptation of Western Asiatic and Egyptian ideas and construction but employs the native means and proportions. Taken from Egypt is the central palace courtyard, but Cretan courts are more rectangular in shape, being twice as long on the north/south axis as on the east/west in order to gain the maximum sunshine in winter.

Palace of King Minos at Knossos

There were several periods of building here and they continued over a long time. The palace was originally excavated by Sir Arthur Evans, who was responsible for much reconstruction work. The palace was a remarkable construction covering nearly five acres. It was destroyed by fire, earthquake and invasion, like the other palaces of Crete, about 1400 B.C., and was not rebuilt. After this time the Minoan civilisation dwindled and the Mycenaean predominated.

The principal living rooms of the palace have been excavated and show the royal apartments grouped round the courtyard, which measures some 180 by 90 feet. The apartments were of several storeys, reached by stairways and the whole palace was interconnected by innumerable passages and stairs. The main palace entrance was on the south side, approached by a paved road, which crossed a ravine spanned by a large viaduct pierced to allow water passage. The external façade, like most Cretan designs, was stepped back sharply, especially on the west side. Walls were of rubble and brick with stucco facing and, near the base, faced with stone slabs. Apart from the royal apartments with their throne room suites and grand staircase there are also a number of halls, two other courts and many smaller rooms. One of the finest apartments is the

Hall of the Double Axes (so called because of the two-bladed axe carved repeatedly on the walls). This was a ground floor room with another hall above. It was colonnaded and open at both ends and could be divided into two rooms in winter by the fitting of four double doors. The two rooms, measuring 18 by 26 feet were then heated by charcoal braziers. The palace was fitted with a drainage system of terracotta pipes, bathroom and toilets, which had water closets with wooden seats. Throughout were magnificent painted ceilings and walls of which fragments remain although for the most part they have been taken to museums for safety (**1, 2** and **3**).

These peoples built citadels on carefully chosen sites, protected by cyclopean walls and fortified gates. Inside the walls were constructed the palace and other important buildings. The citadel of Mycenae itself is a clear example of such patterns for living. Smaller than the palace of Knossos it illustrates nevertheless the architectural layout and typical mode of life of these peoples. The Mycenaeans were seafaring peoples and took over the Minoan trade connections with Egypt. Their methods of building show a more advanced understanding of engineering principles than hitherto and illustrate something of the monumentality of Egyptian work.

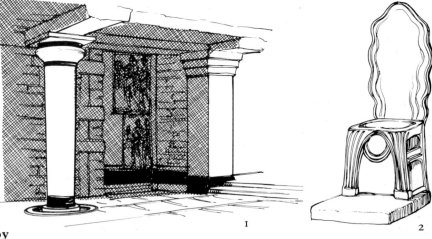

1 Palace of Knossos,
The South Propylaeum,
1775–1580 B.C.
2 Minoan Throne
3 Grand Staircase

Troy

The Trojan civilisation on the coast of Asia Minor is a different branch of development as it owes much of its culture to the interior of Asia Minor rather than the Aegean area and its influence spread only to neighbouring islands. Like Mycenae it was also originally excavated by Schliemann, who doggedly persisted in his search for the city of Homeric legend despite the scepticism of his day. The buildings now excavated cover the period *c.* 2700 B.C. to the Sack of Troy in *c.* 1200. There is a palace with much interesting work surviving and, in the rest of the citadel, fortifications and houses.

Mycenae

The Minoan civilisation spread to the mainland and, with an intermingling of peoples from Asia Minor and the north, provided the nucleus for a new culture around Mycenae in the Peloponnese.

The *citadel of Mycenae* is built on a small hill situated between two larger hills which rise above the plain of Argos near to the sea and the present day port of Nauplia. The citadel (**4**) was rebuilt about 1350 B.C. and is surrounded by walls of cyclopean* masonry in limestone boulders. The walls are 20–25 feet high and the upper courses are of sun-dried brick. At Mycenae there are also walls of fitted polygonal and square stones without mortar. The road from the plain winds up to the fortified main entrance, called the *Lion Gate*. The name is derived from the carved sculpture on the triangular relieving slab† above the lintel wherein are depicted two lions in bold relief, one each side of a column. The heads, which would have faced the visitor to the citadel were separate blocks dowelled in and have disappeared. The lions' paws rest on a plinth. The

* *The term originated from the attitude of the Greeks, who found it difficult to believe that such vast blocks had been erected by man and attributed the construction to the mythical Cyclopes.*

† *The relieving or discharging arch or slab is constructed to prevent the weight above from crushing the lintel stone. Thus, in Mycenaean architecture both the arch and lintel form of construction was employed. It is thought that the triangular relieving arch came from Egypt as it is not known in Minoan architecture.*

column, like most Minoan and Mycenaean designs, tapers slightly towards the bottom. Its capital consists of a square abacus, an echinus and decoration of a row of circular disks. This is probably the most ancient carved sculpture in Europe* and the progenitor of pediment sculpture in Hellenic Greece. The gateway itself is constructed with two vertical jamb blocks and, horizontally across the top of these, a vast lintel block, all of dressed ashlar conglomerate. The lintel stone measures 15 by 7 by 3 feet and is estimated to weigh 20 tons. The doorway is 10 feet high and the sides incline inwards slightly towards the top. It had two wooden doors which

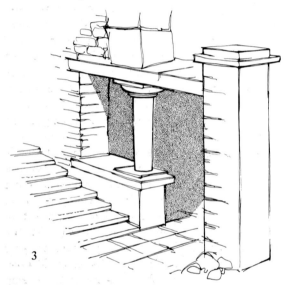

3

opened inwards and folded against the wall; the fitting holes are still visible (**5**).

After passing through the Lion Gate the visitor ascends a ramp and staircase to reach the palace which was constructed on top of the citadel. The ramp winds backwards and forwards to reach the top while the staircase provides a short cut. The *palace* is laid out on Minoan lines with a great court (which had a patterned floor and walls) and a megaron suite leading off it wherein the bases of the columns are still visible. Most of the rooms here were two-storeyed. Part of the megaron has now fallen into the ravine at the edge of the citadel, but the hearth with its raised rim is extant and was originally in the centre of the 40 feet square room. Much of the grand staircase leading down to a lower level can still be seen. A sketch plan of these rooms and a drawing of the staircase as it is today are illus-

** Another old and impressive sculptural scheme is the Lion Terrace on the sacred Isle of Delos (**plate 1**)*

trated in Figs. **7** and **8**. On the north side of the citadel there is a gate in the fortified wall now called the *postern gate* (**6**) which has a triangular shaped roof and which leads towards a secret cistern outside the walls. The vault of this tunnel is formed in the triangular shape, as at Tyrins, with large stones. The exit is composed of horizontally bedded large stones each projecting slightly in front of the one below. This is typical of Mycenaean arches, none of which has radiating voussoirs.

Tholos tombs at Mycenae

These tombs are found primarily in the Peloponnese and consist of underground circular chambers covered with a mound of earth and approached by means of a dromos, which is a stone-faced passage. Inside, the tomb is faced with squared blocks of masonry set in horizontal courses which are corbelled to meet at a domed centre overhead. Such tombs are constructed by first cutting the open passage (dromos) into the hillside until the ground is rising high enough above it. After the last burial the dromos is filled in. Only the mound of earth is then visible and the tomb would last as long as the vault withheld the water from the earth above. Good examples have buttress walls encircling the vault to protect it and take the thrust. The best and most famous tholos tomb at Mycenae is that known as the *Treasury of Atreus* built *c.* 1330 B.C. This is finely constructed with dressed and curved, conglomerate blocks. Inside the dome each block overlaps and counterweighs the one below on a cantilever system. The blocks are wedge-shaped and the interstices are filled with clay and stone. The chamber is $47\frac{1}{2}$ feet in diameter and is 43 feet high. Its interior is intact except that the decoration has been removed. There is a rock cut chamber at one side with its own doorway. The dromos approach is 120 feet long and 20 feet wide and its side walls, made of blocks of dressed grey conglomerate, are regularly laid and rise in steps towards the doorway. This doorway is 18 feet high and inclines inwards, Egyptian fashion, while the entrance itself also slants inwards. The lintel blocks, inner and outer, are gigantic (each 26 by 16 by 4 feet and weighing 100 tons) and extend across into the walls of the dromos. The relieving triangle above is now empty, but originally it had a decorated faced slab parts of which, with the original flanking columns of green limestone, are now in the British Museum (**59, 60**). The columns, decorated by scroll pattern, are slender and taper towards the base. The doorway passage is paved with limestone slabs and there was originally a double wooden door (**10, 12**). This tomb, like that of Clytemnestra and others, was built for the burial of a king and his family. Tombs for other people were cut into the rock.

Citadel of Tiryns

The ruins here are of an early palace built on a ridge rising from the Argos plain nearer to the sea than Mycenae. Much of the citadel walls remain as does the layout of the palace on top of the acropolis. The cyclopean masonry is particularly large scale and well built. There are different periods of work here from *c.* 1400 to *c.* 1280. The palace itself was built in the thirteenth century B.C. and was of sun-dried brick with wooden columns. The most interesting remains are a long gallery which is covered along its entire length by large stones horizontally bedded to form a triangular shaped roof and this is in a good state of preservation (**9**). There is also a little postern gate nearby of similar construction (**11**).

These great Mycenaean settlements were destroyed by fire in about 1100 B.C., but the knowledge of them and their people lived on by word of mouth. The Homeric poems describe a picture of Mycenaean life—the age of Agamemnon, Clytemnestra and Troy—distorted by time and repetition but basically true. The Mycenaeans were conquered, it is believed, by the northern Dorians, but it is not yet established how close their connection was with their inheritors, the Greeks. Classical Greece was chiefly peopled by Dorians (centre Sparta) and Ionians (Athens) who were descendants of the Pelasgi.

Classical and Hellenistic Greece
c. 700–146 B.C.

Several centuries passed between the collapse of Bronze Age Mycenaean architecture and the rise of Hellenic art; a period of 'Dark Ages' ensued, and when Hellenic architecture evolved it was different from the work of its predecessors. The Greeks were strongly influenced by maritime contact with their neighbours: Egypt, Assyria and Persia. Their massive Doric Order, always the Greek favourite, has much of Egyptian monumentality in it as has their art something of the Assyrian richness of detail. Colour was as important to them as to all peoples who live in a sunny climate and they used it to adorn both exteriors and interiors of their buildings; this is a fact not always realised when studying the weathered ruins extant today. Indeed, both effort and knowledge are required in order to understand Greek architecture from these ruined buildings. None of them is intact; the sculpture has been almost entirely removed to museums; the wood and metal parts are missing and, most important from the viewpoint of appreciating the original appearance, they are roofless so that light enters where shadow once was and the whole balance of form is altered. It is a tribute, therefore, to the perfection of Greek form in building that these ruins should appear so satisfying and so moving to twentieth century beholders. The prime feature of Greek architecture is its intellectual quality. The Greeks did not create a variety of design or show great inventiveness or a desire for innovation. They developed to an intensely high degree a standard of perfection for the designs which they evolved. As the most important Greek buildings were temples (rather than palaces and tombs as in Minoan architecture), every effort was made to develop the finest possible harmony of their different parts and proportion and line of these individually and collectively. This ideal was pursued relentlessly by architects and artists who were not satisfied with less than perfection. This standard was reached at the zenith of the Hellenic style in the fifth century B.C. where buildings such as the Parthenon even today illustrate to the most uninformed beholder the intellectual beauty of line and proportion which can only be the result in human endeavour of tremendous study, effort and knowledge.

Greek architecture belongs to three chief periods: the archaic, up to about 480 B.C.; the early classical of the fifth and fourth centuries and the later Hellenistic from then until the Roman Conquest in 146 B.C. Their buildings included temples, theatres, stadia, agora, stoas, tombs, town fortifications, gymnasia and treasuries. Of

CITADEL AND PALACE OF MYCENAE

4 LION GATE — PALACE

ENTRANCE

5

6

7

THRONE ROOM

GREAT COURT

PORCH OF THE MEGARON

VESTIBULE

MEGARON

HEARTH

ANTE-ROOM

DRAIN

CLIFF

8

GRAND STAIRCASE

4 *General view of citadel, c. 1350 B.C.*
5 *The Lion Gate*
6 *The Postern Gate*

7 *The Grand Staircase*
8 *Simplified sketch plan of the layout of the principal palace rooms*

these the most common remains are of temples and theatres, though the latter were, almost without exception, altered in Roman times. Ancient Greece extended beyond the mainland and surrounding islands and remains of Greek buildings are found today in the Greek colonies of Sicily, Southern Italy and in Asia Minor. As the prime building material of Greece was marble, many of these buildings have endured without great surface damage until today. Their damage is due primarily to earthquake and destruction by man. Greek marble is of high quality and the Greeks so admired its fineness of surface grain that in areas such as southern Italy where limestone was used for building, as at Paestum, they made a stucco of powdered marble and coated the limestone to provide their usual high standard of finish. Greek architecture was suited to the climate and mode of life which was outdoor in character. Colonnades supported porticoes and roofs and these supplied shelter from the hot sun and sudden rainstorms but also cool air in their shade. Windows were unimportant but doorways were finely proportioned, simply designed and rectangular in shape. The style of architecture was mainly a trabeated form and composed of horizontal blocks upon columns and walls. Vaults and arches were comparatively rare and roofs were generally of timber and tiled above. Archaic work was severe and stark, generally with heavy columns and capitals. Gradually refinements were made and proportions became more elegant though still robust in construction. In fifth and fourth century work, for example, stability was increased as well as refinement achieved by extreme care in the fitting of blocks especially in columns and walls. Surfaces were rubbed down to fit perfectly and there was no need of mortar.

Greek Town Plans

Many Greek cities were built on natural hills and were surrounded by walls with fortified gates and towers. Remains of these fortifications exist as, for example, at *Syracuse* in Sicily where Dionysios built his forts and walls in the fourth century B.C. for protection against the Carthaginians. The city upon the hill was called the acropolis (a literal translation of this conception) and the principal buildings of the city were inside these walls on top of the hill, while most of the houses were outside. Credit for invention of the orderly city plan on gridiron pattern is given by Aristotle to *Hippodamus of Miletus* who laid out *Piraeus*, the port of Athens, in the mid-fifth century. Streets were straight and wide and crossed one another at right angles. This is a pattern adopted later by the Romans and, in our own times, by the French and the Americans. Hippodamus had also planned the city of *Miletus* in Asia Minor about 470–466 which contained some hundreds of rectangular blocks in its layout. The central area was reserved for the agora and stoas, where business and commerce were carried out, while residential areas surrounded it. Other cities on similar lines were *Priene, Pergamon, Ephesos* and *Corinth*.

The Orders

All the countries in Europe as well as those in the New World have, for long periods in their architectural history, used a system of orders in classical architecture, a system first devised by the Greeks, adapted by the Romans and revived in Renaissance Europe. It is a formula which has survived for some 2500 years and was still being used, in modified form, in architecture of the earlier twentieth century. The term 'order' is given to the three styles in Greek architecture: Doric, Ionic and Corinthian. Each order consists of an upright *column* or support which has a *base* (optional) and *capital* and the horizontal lintel supported by it. This last member, called the *entablature*, is divided into three parts; the lowest member is the *architrave*, the centre member the *frieze* and at the top the *cornice*. Each order possesses specific relative proportions between its parts, also certain distinguishing features and mouldings peculiar to itself. The size of a building does not affect these proportions, which remain constant, and differing scale does not impair the perfection of such proportions. The Greeks never used a part of one order with a part of another or, except rarely, employed more than one order on a building façade though they might use one for the exterior and another for the interior. The proportions of the orders were developed by trial and error over a long period of time. Earlier examples of the seventh and sixth centuries have massive columns,

TIRYNS AND MYCENAE

9 *The Gallery, Tiryns, thirteenth century B.C.*
10 *Treasury of Atreus, Mycenae, Interior of doorway,*
   c. 1330 B.C.

11 *Gateway to gallery wall, Tiryns*
12 *Treasury of Atreus, Mycenae, Exterior of doorway.*
   Columns and decoration restored as in British Museum

GREEK CLASSICAL ORDERS AND DETAIL

13 The Doric Order, The Parthenon, Athens,
   447–432 B.C.
14 The Ionic Order, the Erechtheion, Athens,
   421–405 B.C.
15 The Corinthian Order, the Monument of Lysicrates,
   c. 334 B.C.

16 Ionic capital, Delphi
17 Ionic base, Delphi
18 Entablature, Tholos to Minerva, Delphi, c. 390 B.C.
19 Corinthian capital, the Olympieion, Athens,
   begun 174 B.C.

20 *Minoan Column at Eleusis*
21 *Base, the Erechtheion, Athens, 421–405 B.C.*
22 *Ionic capital, Erechtheion*
23 *The Parthenon, Athens, 437–432 B.C. (restored)*
24 *Ionic base, Temple of Athena Nike, Athens,*
    427–424 B.C.

25 *Ionic capital, Temple of Artemis, Ephesus, mid-sixth*
    century
26 *Order, porch of the Tower of the Winds, Athens,*
    c. 40 B.C. (restored)
27 *Corinthian capital, Tholos at Epidauros, c. 360 B.C.*
28 *Proto-Ionic capital, Larisa, Asia Minor, early sixth*
    century

capitals and entablatures, and the intercolumniations were narrow. Mouldings and curved forms became more refined as time passed. A clear example of this process can be seen by comparing the echinus in a Doric capital from the temples at *Paestum* or *Agrigento* with those of the *Parthenon* (**23, 48** and **50**). The former are more bulbous and semi-circular in section, the latter are of a most subtle, flattish silhouette. The Greeks preferred the Doric Order and used it particularly for large buildings and for exterior façades. The Ionic Order is seen more in eastern colonial areas, especially in Asia Minor and Aegean islands.

The Doric Order

This is the most massive of the Greek orders and the one upon which the Greeks lavished the most care. The columns are placed close together and have no bases but stand directly upon a three-step stylobate. As in all Greek orders the shaft is fluted in shallow, subtle curved sections divided by sharp arrises. The number of flutes per column varies; in the ideal design like the *Parthenon* there are 20, but a greater or smaller number is used according to material and proportion; for example, at *Paestum* in the *Temple of Hera* there are 24 while in the *Temple of Poseidon* at *Sounion* only 16. Including the capital, the column has a height of four to six-and-a-half times the base diameter, and, in general, the earlier the building the thicker the column. The *capital* itself consists of a square *abacus* at the top and below this a curved *echinus* and annular rings. The *entablature*, usually about a quarter the height of the order, has a plain *architrave* and a *cornice* which projects strongly and under whose soffit are flat blocks called *mutules*, set one over each triglyph and one between, which have each 18 *guttae* in three rows beneath. The *frieze* of the Doric Order is distinctive; it is divided into *triglyphs* and *metopes*. The triglyphs, each of which has vertical channels carved in it, are placed one over each column and one between except at the angles where, the columns being closer together, the external triglyph is placed at the extreme end of the frieze and not over the centre of the angle column. The metopes are the spaces between, rectangular in early examples and square in later ones. These are commonly decorated with sculptural groups, as in the

Parthenon, so many of whose metopes are in the British Museum or the Louvre (PLATE 2). These metope sculptures together with the pedimental groups constitute the glory of the Doric Order which epitomises the ideal union of simple, perfectly proportioned architectural masses with sculptural decoration. The frieze is separated from the architrave by a narrow band called the *regula* with six guttae beneath each triglyph (**13, 18, 23** and PLATE 4).

The Ionic Order

This order is in general a later development than the Doric but early prototypes have been found, particularly in Asia Minor from where the Aeolian capital (from Aeolis in north-west Asia Minor) stems. This has two volutes with palmette between, flattened to fit the architrave. Below, the echinus is formed by a water-lily shape. This design is related to both Egyptian and Syrian capitals (**28**). The true Ionic capital dates from the late sixth century and has two scroll *volutes*, based upon a shell formation or that of an animal's horns, which face the front elevation, while below is an *echinus moulding* with egg and dart enrichment. The *necking* or astragal is sometimes, as in the Erechtheion, decorated by anthemion relief design. The order is differently proportioned from the Doric; it has a much slenderer column, of height about nine diameters, carved into 24 flutes of semi-circular section separated by fillets not arrises and it is completed by a moulded base which is also often carved. The *entablature* is narrower in depth, generally one-fifth of the whole order, and has an architrave set forward in a three plane, triple fascia, a frieze without triglyphs or metopes but often decorated by a continuous band of sculpture, for example, the Erechtheion, and a cornice of smaller projection than the Doric, without mutules, but generally with dentil ornament surmounted by a corona and cyma recta moulding. The order is graceful and well proportioned and was used by the Greeks for smaller buildings, interiors and, commonly, in Asia Minor (**14, 16, 17, 21, 22, 24, 25, 28** and PLATE 5).

The Corinthian Order

This order was used much less by the Greeks

Plate 3
The Acropolis of Athens viewed from the Hill of Filoppapos. Below the theatre, behind the
Hill of Lycabettos

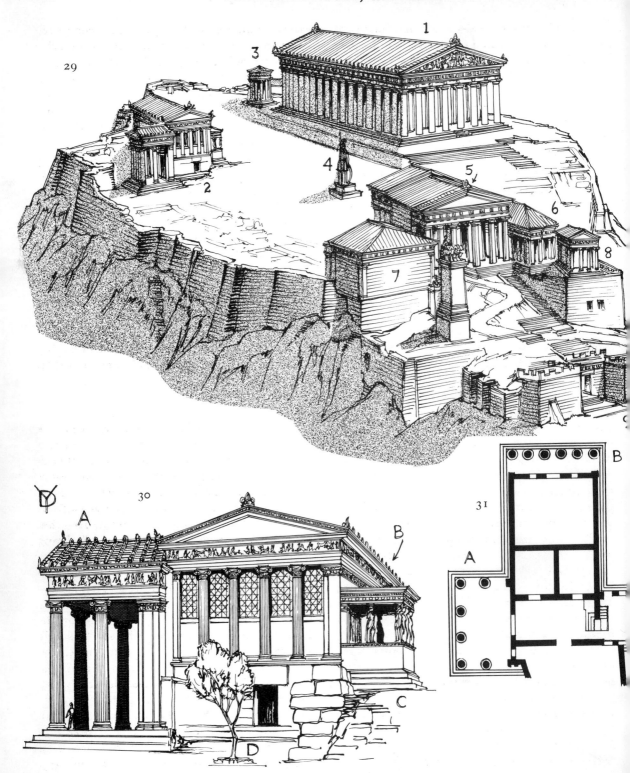

29 *Sketch showing restoration of the principal buildings*
of the Acropolis, viewed from the west.
  1) The Parthenon
  2) The Erechtheion
  3) Ionic Tholos
  4) Statue of Athena Promachos by Pheidias
  5) The Propylaea

  6) Southern wing of propylaea
  7) North wing of propylaea, the picture gallery
  8) Temple of Athena Niké
  9) Main entrance to Acropolis
30 *The Erechtheion (restoration), viewed from west,*
     421–405 B.C.
31 *Plan, Erechtheion*

than the other two orders and not many examples survive. The most common design, that adopted by the Romans, was similar to the Ionic Order in base, column and entablature, was richly ornamented and had a deeper cornice. The chief difference between the orders was in the *capital*, which was deep and had a four-faced abacus identical on all four sides. The capital below the abacus was in the form of a concave bell decorated by two tiers of acanthus leaves above which rose corner volutes supporting the angles of the abacus and central caulicoli or volutes also (**15, 19** and **27**). Another type of design had one row of acanthus leaves and, above these, a row of lotus or palm leaves with no volutes (**26**).

Building Materials and Methods

In early times the Greeks used sun-dried bricks, terracotta, wood and stone. Later, stone and marble were the chief *materials*; limestone and conglomerate were generally coated in marble stucco. Most of the temples in Greece itself are in marble which was used from *c.* 600 B.C. The best known marbles are Pentelic from Mount Pentelicus near Athens, Hymettian from Mount Hymettos also near Athens, Parian from the island of Paros and Eleusian from Eleusis. Pentelic marble is dazzling white and weathers well, as can be seen by the temples on the Acropolis in Athens even today. Hymettian marble is also white but has grey-blue markings; Parian is used predominantly for sculpture while Eleusian marble, as evidenced in the frieze of the Erechtheion, is dark grey and was used as a contrast material. Stone was more usual in the provinces, particularly in Italy and Sicily.

We have a good knowledge of *Greek building methods* in stone and marble from ruined remains, quarries and building inscriptions. The Greeks rarely used mortar but fitted their blocks with meticulous care, using metal dowels and cramps of bronze or iron set in molten lead to hold the blocks in position. This method is presumed to have been employed because of the earthquake hazard in the area. In particular, the drums of the columns were finely fitted so that the joints were barely visible even on close inspection. Bosses (ancons) were left on the sides of the drums for manipulation, as can be seen in the unfinished *Temple* at *Segesta* (**51**). Column flutes were

carved from top and bottom then completed when the column was *in situ*. Stone and marble walls were built in large blocks, without mortar, and the lowest course was generally twice as high as the others. Sometimes hollow wall construction was used in order to reduce weight or economise in material. Greek architecture is of lintel construction and the Greeks were slow or unwilling to develop new structural methods: they preferred to perfect their existing ones. This is particularly noticeable with regard to the arch and the vault—constructional means which the Romans were later to exploit. Greek roofing was by timber and the roof pitch was low (anything else being unnecessary in the Greek climate). Thus the pitch of the end pediments was determined by this rake and this gave the beautiful proportions which Greek pediments possess; comparison with Renaissance examples in Western Europe brings out this quality. The roof rafters were then covered by terracotta or marble tiles and interior ceilings were of coffered marble.

Refinements

These refinements of line, mass and curve are the factors that make all the difference between a good Greek building and a bad one and between the Greek original and the later Renaissance interpretation. The refinements used in the greatest periods of Greek architecture are so subtle as to be barely visible to the casual eye; indeed that is their chief purpose—to make the building appear correctly delineated and not curved, and to give it vitality and plasticity. The true horizontal or vertical line, particularly when silhouetted against a brilliant blue sky, appears concave to the human eye and, to offset this illusion the Greeks created a convex line and form so subtly and meticulously worked out as to appear to create a straight vertical or horizontal. Thus, taking the *Parthenon* as the finest illustration, all horizontal and vertical lines are in fact curved to counteract this visual illusion. This curvature applies to the stylobate (rise of $4\frac{1}{4}$ inches in a length of 228 feet, the entablature (curve 1 in 600), the columns (slanting inwards 1 in 150), and to the pediment. Columns diminish in diameter from bottom to top and, in addition, have an entasis whose widest point is about one third the way up from the base. Each flute curves in tune with the general entasis, which is to the order of about three-quarters of an inch to a height of 34 feet. In the Parthenon, the peristyle columns have a diameter of six feet two inches at base and four feet two inches just below the capital. Ionic and Corinthian columns, however, taper much less; in the *Erechtheion*, for instance, the difference is only six inches between the bottom and the top diameters. Also the inter-columniation (or column spacing) varies; the outside columns are closer together than the intermediate ones. At the Parthenon the differ-ence is two feet, from a six foot intercolumniation on exterior columns to eight feet elsewhere. Angle columns are also generally wider than their neighbours; this is because a silhouetted column appears narrower than one against a light back-ground. All the columns incline slightly inwards, as do the faces of the entablature and pediments, in order to lend a pyramidal form to the building. These refinements were costly to produce at their highest level and thus it is only such buildings as those on the Acropolis at the zenith of Greek architecture which achieved such a standard. These refinements are aesthetic in purpose as well as corrective, but since they are so subtly carried out the cost is proportionately great. On the Parthenon, for example, none of the correc-tions are arcs of circles but parabolae corrected down to the smallest members such as abaci.

Temples

The most important form in Greek architecture was the temple which was built not to house worshippers but the deity. The earliest examples were based upon the design of the Minoan megaron in the Bronze Age palaces and consisted of rectangular halls with frontal porches sup-ported on columns. The Greek desire for symmetry then created a porch at each end and enclosed a central naos or room to house the cult statue and later another smaller room behind to act as a treasury. From these beginnings evolved the varied designs of temple. However, even in the fifth century the variation in temples was not so much in form as in detail; they remained rectangular in shape, containing naos and trea-sury and with a portico each end and a surround-ing colonnade. According to whether the temple was large or small the number of columns

differed. Smaller temples had only four columns in their porticoes (tetrastyle form), larger examples had six (hexastyle), eight (octastyle), nine (nonastyle) or ten (decastyle). In each instance there were generally twice as many columns in the lateral peristyle as in the front and rear. The *Parthenon*, for example, is octastyle and has 17 columns at each side. All temples were raised on a platform (stylobate), generally of three steps. The entrance door was usually in the centre of the east wall behind the portico columns and designed so that the sunlight would fall upon the cult statue in the naos. Windows were rare. Light was admitted through the doorways or roof sky lights. Roofs were not flat but low pitched, with a ridge pole. The triangular space at each end of the temple was closed by a wall (tympanum) and protected by a raking cornice. The pedimental tympanum was generally filled with sculpture. The rafters were covered by tiles and these terminated at the sides in an antefix or gutter. Waterspouts, often in the form of lion's heads, were set at intervals to let out rain water. Acroteria decorated the three angles of the pediment.

Temples were designed for external effect, for the worshippers remained outside round the altar. Thus the naos was plain and solidly walled while the sculptural and painted decoration was on the exterior. It was usually confined to the pediments, frieze and acroteria. In large temples where the width of the naos was too great to be spanned by beams, interior columns were used to make nave and aisles. These were in two tiers and supported galleries over the aisles and the roof. Most of these second tier columns have vanished except in such examples as the *Temple of Hera* at *Paestum* (**44**) and the *Temple of Aphaia, Aegina* (see restored illustration **42**).

Temples on the Acropolis of Athens

Many Greek cities contained a hill which was the defensible part and where the important build-ings were constructed. In Athens there was an ideal natural hill with only one side, the west, which could be approached easily. It was in-habited by succeeding generations, but the ruined temples which now adorn it date principally from the fifth century when Athens, under the leadership of Pericles, experienced its great epoch (**29** and PLATE 3).

The Parthenon 447–432 B.C.

This temple, magnificent even in ruin, dominates the Athenian acropolis and is the finest of all Greek temples, marking the climax of the Doric style. The Parthenon had survived in good condition until 1687, when it was partially destroyed by an explosion during the Turko-Venetian war. From drawings made before this date we have a clear idea of what the pedimental sculptures looked like *in situ*. After the explosion the ruins deteriorated rapidly and in 1801–3 Lord Elgin removed much of the sculpture of the pediments, metopes and frieze to England, where it is at present beautifully displayed in the British Museum. It is a fallacy to suppose that Lord Elgin stole these sculptures or at least acquired them in a transaction of doubtful honesty. He was given formal permission by the lawful government of Greece (then the Turkish Empire) to remove the works. He did so with greatest care and later sold them to the British Museum for a much smaller sum than he had already spent. He had no means of knowing that Greece would become independent once more and if he had not acted when he did the sculpture would soon have suffered irreparable damage from neglect. Whether the British Museum or the Louvre should now return such work to Greece is another question.

The Parthenon was built of Pentelic marble on a limestone foundation over the site of an earlier temple. The architects were *Ictinus* and *Callicrates* and the chief sculptor *Pheidias*. It was the largest temple on the Greek mainland and had a peristyle of 17 lateral columns and octastyle porticoes. There was a naos which had interior columns on two storeys also a back chamber, presumably for use as a treasury. The temple was dedicated to the city's patron goddess Athena and was built on the highest part of the acropolis so that it was visible from the town. Near the west end of the naos stood the famous statue of Athena by Pheidias, made in gold and ivory and standing 40 feet high. Today the most prominent external features are the peristyle columns of which 32 still stand on their stylobate. The temple is so beautifully proportioned and refined that it is difficult, on sight, to realise its immense size, particularly as there is no other large building in the vicinity to give scale. In fact the columns are over 34 feet high and measure six feet two inches in diameter at base. The visitor only realises this when, sitting down gratefully on the stylobate for a rest in the shade after climbing up the acropolis, he leans his back against a column and finds that his shoulders neatly fit into one flute from arris to arris (**23, 29, 33** and **34**). Apart from the beauty of the Pentelic marble and the design and craftsmanship of the Parthenon, its finest feature was its sculpture which, under the leadership of Pheidias, was of the highest quality of work by the greatest age of sculptors that Europe has so far produced. The two pediments represent, at the east end the Birth of Athena and at the west, the contest between Athena and Poseidon for Attica. A little of this work is *in situ*, the rest is in the British Museum, the Louvre and the Athens Museum. The metopes are about four feet five inches square and contained high relief sculpture which was originally brightly coloured (PLATE 2). The masterpiece of the Parthenon sculptures was the frieze which ran all round the temple inside the peristyle and high on the naos and porch walls. It was nearly 524 feet long and beautifully executed. Parts of it remain *in situ* but are difficult to see as the frieze is 40 feet above the ground and, owing to the narrow floor space between the naos wall and peristyle columns, one cannot step back to admire it. Indeed, it is much easier, if less moving, to view the long sections in the British Museum (PLATES 9 and 10). In order to assist the viewer from below the frieze was designed at an angle so that, while the face surface is vertical, the background tilts forward towards the top giving higher relief to the heads than feet (PLATE 4).

The Erechtheion 421–405 B.C.

This is the best building in the Ionic order in Greece and is famed for its quality rather than its size. It stands on the acropolis north of the Parthenon on a sloping site; this factor, and because it housed three deities, account for its unusual plan. There are three façades, east, north and south, all at different levels. The eastern part was dedicated to Athena, guardian of the city; the ground slopes downwards towards the west where there is a basement room, with access on the west façade, while above this small doorway are four Ionic columns with bronze latticed windows between. The north porch is a large

Plate 4 Doric capital, Parthenon, Athens, 447–432 B.C.

Plate 5 Ionic capital, Temple of Artemis, Sardis, Turkey

Plate 6
The Erechtheion, Athens, 421–405 B.C.

BUILDINGS ON THE ACROPOLIS, ATHENS, FIFTH CENTURY

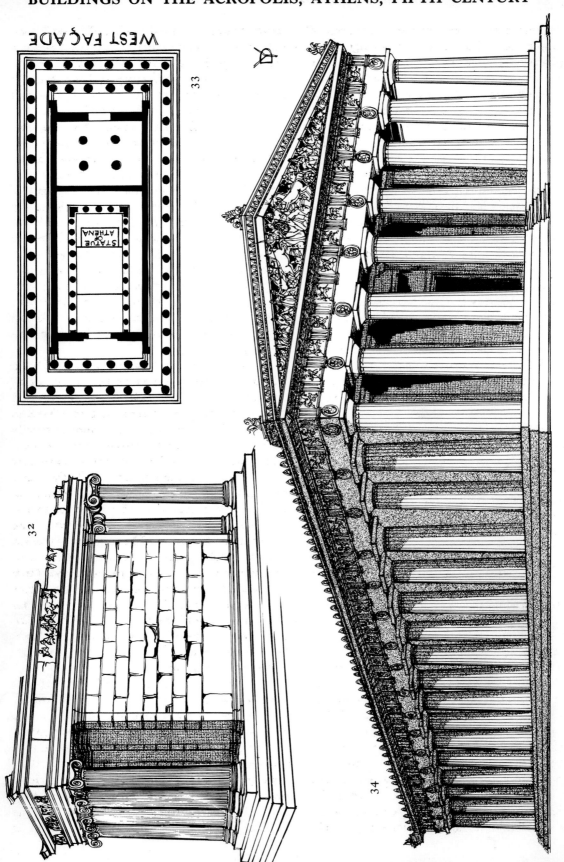

WEST FAÇADE

STATUE OF ATHENA

32   Temple of Athena Nike, 427–424 B.C.
33   Plan of Parthenon
34   The Parthenon from the north-west (restored), 447–432 B.C.

Ionic entrance and stands at the lowest level of the temple. Behind this portico is a magnificent carved doorway. The whole porch contains the highest quality of Greek decorative carving as can be seen in the capitals, bases and doorway details (**21, 22** and **65**). The south porch, on higher ground, has the six caryatid figures, each seven feet nine inches high, standing on a marble plinth and supporting a marble entablature and roof. The three western figures take their weight on the right leg, the eastern on the left (PLATE 11). The Erechtheion is built of Pentelic marble and was designed by *Mnesicles*. The decoration throughout is varied and shows exquisite detail and craftmanship; this is particularly apparent in the anthemion and guilloche ornament. The pediments are plain but the frieze of dark grey Eleusian marble was originally decorated its full length by white marble sculptured figures and animals attached by metal cramps. Gilt and colour were used also. The interior was destroyed when the building was converted into a church and later into a Turkish harem (**14, 21, 22, 29, 30, 31, 65, 67** and PLATE 6).

Temple of Athena Nike (Nike Apteros) 427–424 B.C.

This tiny building erected near the propylaea on the acropolis was designed by *Callicrates*. It consists of a single naos with four Ionic columns front and back and stands on a stylobate. It is only 23 feet high but beautifully proportioned and had some fine sculpture on the pediments and on the frieze, some of which remains (**32**).

Temples in Greece

Temples in or near Athens

The most complete Greek temple is that built on rising ground above the Athenian agora called the *Temple of Hephaistos* or the *Theseion*. Like the Parthenon it is of Pentelic marble, of similar date *c.* 449 B.C. and is in the Doric order. It has six columns to each portico and 13 lateral columns. The building was damaged by fire in A.D. 267; it originally had two storeys both in the Doric order but its inner colonnade was destroyed when the temple was made into a church in the fifth century A.D. and it was given solid walls and a barrel vaulted roof. Its preservation probably resulted from this solid roofing. The sculpture, in Parian marble, consisted of high relief metopes illustrating the exploits of Theseus and a continuous frieze two feet eight inches high under the porticoes. Some of the metopes and the east end frieze are still *in situ* (**35** and **36**).

On a central space amidst the speeding traffic of Athens stand the 16 Corinthian columns which are all that remain of the immense temple of the *Olympeion* begun in 174 B.C. Dedicated to Olympian Zeus, it was built on the stylobate of an earlier Doric temple. It was designed by *Cossutius*, a Roman citizen, but whose work was essentially Greek. This enormous temple measured 135 by 354 feet and stood in a precinct (still marked out) 424 by 680 feet. The columns, each 56 feet high, are of Pentelic marble and have slender shafts and finely carved Corinthian capitals. It had a double colonnade of 20 lateral columns and three rows of eight columns at each end (**19** and **43**).

The Doric *Temple of Poseidon* (440 B.C.) has a magnificent site on the high southerly promontory of Attica at *Cape Sounion*. The white local marble columns can be seen for great distances especially from the sea. There were originally pedimental sculptures but no sculptured metopes. The columns, which have no entasis, have only 16 flutes to offset their slenderness. On the island of *Aegina*, the *Temple of Aphaia* also stands on a fine site on a ridge visible for miles out to sea. This hexastyle temple was built of limestone coated in marble stucco. The sculpture, of which a considerable quantity has been found, is in Parian marble. That from the pediments (now in a Munich museum) is an interesting example of late archaic work of about 480 B.C. Roof tiles on the temple were of marble and terracotta; those at the edge were of marble carved with lion's head water-spouts. There were fine antifixae and acroteria (**42**).

On a number of different sites on the *Greek mainland* and in the *Peloponnese*, Olympia, Delphi, Corinth, Epidauros, etc., are the remains of many temples. Most of these are fragmentary though the quality is high and enough remains for the original design to be apparent. Most interesting of these examples, which are all in the Doric order, are the temples at *Olympia*: the very ancient *Temple of Hera c.* 600 B.C. and the *Temple of Zeus c.* 470 B.C.; the *Temple of Apollo* at

THE GREEK AGORA, ATHENS

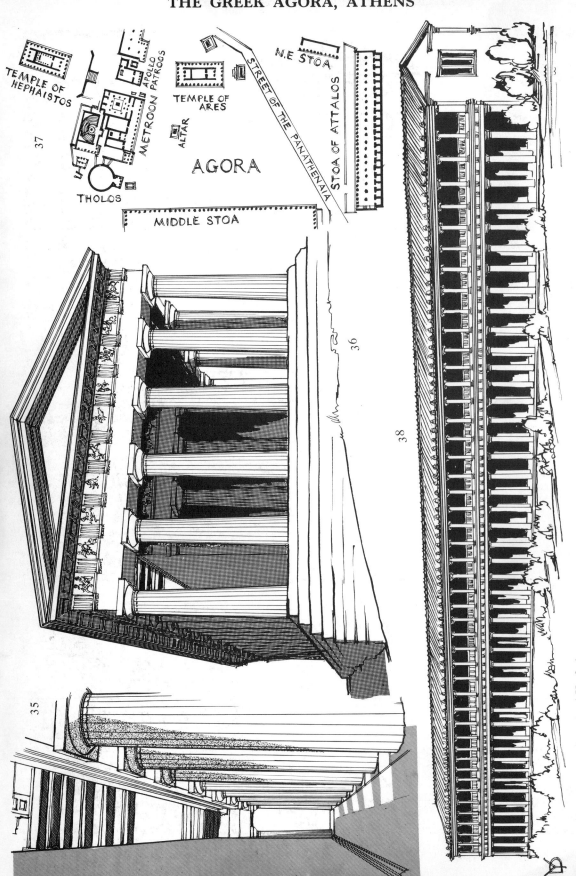

TEMPLE OF
HEPHAISTOS

APOLLO PATROOS

METROON

TEMPLE OF
ARES

ALTAR

AGORA

THOLOS

N.E STOA

STREET OF THE PANATHENAIA

STOA OF ATTALOS

MIDDLE STOA

37

36

38

35

35 Ambulatory, Temple of Hephaistos
36 Temple of Hephaistos, c. 449 B.C.
37 Plan of part of Agora showing these buildings
38 The Stoa of Attalos, c. 150 B.C. Restored 1953–6 by American School of Classical Studies, Athens

BUILDINGS IN OR NEAR ATHENS

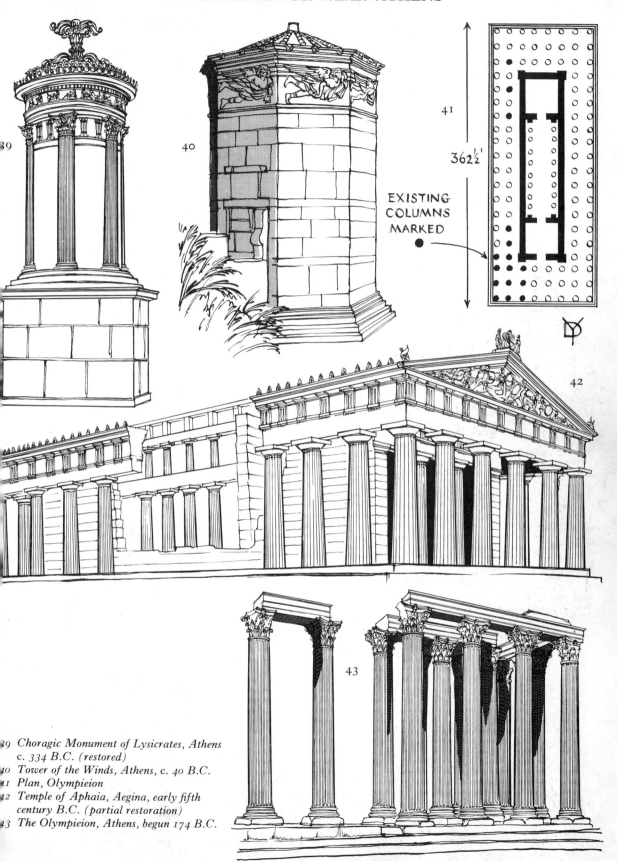

41

362½'

EXISTING
COLUMNS
MARKED

42

43

39 *Choragic Monument of Lysicrates, Athens
c. 334 B.C. (restored)*
40 *Tower of the Winds, Athens, c. 40 B.C.*
41 *Plan, Olympieion*
42 *Temple of Aphaia, Aegina, early fifth
century B.C. (partial restoration)*
43 *The Olympieion, Athens, begun 174 B.C.*

Corinth, also very ancient, sixth century B.C.; the *Temple of Apollo* at *Delphi*, fourth century B.C. and the *Temple of Ascelpios* at *Epidauros*, early fourth century B.C. At *Bassae*, near Andritsaina, in the Peloponnese, is the *Temple of Apollo* built *c.* 450 B.C. in which all three orders are used. It is a hexastyle temple with 15 lateral columns. Parts of the marble frieze and some metopes are in the British Museum. The temple was built in limestone by Ictinus, architect of the Parthenon, with the Doric order used on the exterior, Ionic inside and an early example of Corinthian capitals. These Corinthian remains have been lost, but the design can be perceived from drawings made at the 1811 excavations. They had two rows of small acanthus leaves and, above, pairs of tall leaves and volutes.

Temples in Asia Minor

These temples were mostly Ionic and larger than those in Greece but remains are fragmentary, only one or two columns standing in most instances. The Greek cities of *Ephesos* and *Miletus* contained a number of examples; for instance, the *Temple of Apollo Didymaeus* at *Miletus*, the *Temple of Artemis* at *Ephesos** and the *Temple of Athena Polias* at *Priene*. All of fourth century construction, these temples were large scale and had beautiful sculpture and decoration. There is little left because most of the material has been taken over the centuries to build Byzantine churches and other buildings. Capitals, bases and fragments of sculpture are displayed in European museums.

Doric Temples in Italy and Sicily

Here the remains are fairly complete, indeed much more so than in Greece, and are from early periods of building thus providing a contrasting source for study of the sixth and fifth centuries B.C. and for the differences between colonial architecture here and the more refined work in Greece itself. In *Italy* the chief group of remains is at *Paestum* in Southern Italy south of Salerno (the Greeks called it Poseidonia). There are three temples here of which two are large and in a good state of preservation. The best example is the *Temple of Hera*, popularly called *Temple of Poseidon*, built *c.* 460 B.C. Here all the exterior columns are standing and, inside, both tiers of the two storeys are represented. It is a hexastyle temple, 198 by 80 feet, built in travertine stone and originally coated with marble stucco (**44, 45, 46, 47** and **48**).

In *Sicily* there were a number of Greek centres which have remains of temples and theatres. At *Agrigento*, on the south coast of the island, there are several temples of which the *Temple of Olympian Zeus* is the largest. It was begun in about 485 B.C. but never completed owing to the Carthaginian invasion. Like other temples in Italy and Sicily it is built of coarse stone coated with marble stucco. An interior feature of its design are atlas figures about 25 feet high which probably stood between the columns. Another large *temple* at Agrigento is that of *Concord* which is well preserved probably because it was later converted into a church. It was built about 420 B.C., of local stone, and has complete gables as well as columns (**50**). There are further temples at *Selinunte* and at *Segesta* (**51**) while at *Syracuse* the *Temple of Athena* is now incorporated into the Baroque cathedral. The temple was hexastyle with 36 columns each 28 feet high and stood on a massive podium. In the seventh century A.D. the Byzantine bishop converted the temple into a basilica. Later the Normans further adapted it and in the eighteenth century the church was rebuilt after a series of earthquakes. The Greek temple is still there and 12 of its columns are visible in the north and south aisles of the present cathedral, still standing on their stylobate.

Tholoi

These are circular buildings covered by conical roofs. The form was a common one from early times in Greece, being used for simple dwelling huts, tombs and for other purposes (page 4 and PLATE 7). There is a *tholos* at *Delphi c.* 390 B.C., PARTLY RECONSTRUCTED (**53**), and other examples at *Olympia*, *Epidauros*, the *Athenian agora* and on the *Acropolis* in *Athens* (**29**). The *Delphi tholos* stands upon a stylobate and had an outer ring of 20 Doric columns inside which was the naos wall and inside this again 10 Corinthian columns. The external diameter was 48 feet. The roof over the naos was conical and there was a separate roof over the colonnade sloping at a lower level. This tholos was designed by *Theodorus of Phocaea* who set the pattern for these buildings which was followed by *Polykleitos the Younger* at *Epidauros*. This example, of which little remains, was larger, with an external diameter of 66 feet (**27**).

Other Buildings

Propylaea

The gateway to a sanctuary was sometimes a simple doorway called a propylon but in more important instances was a large construction combining several doorways called propylaea. There are remains of these at *Olympia* and *Epidauros* but the best known example is that at the *Acropolis, Athens*. This magnificent entrance on the western approach to the hill was built by *Mnesicles* from 437–432 B.C. but was never completed owing to the Peloponnesian War. Though roofless, much of it still stands as entrance to the acropolis. The design of Pentelic marble has a central mass with five doorways flanked east and west by a Doric hexastyle portico; the rear one being at a higher level than the former. At the sides, north and south, are wings, the northern wing containing two chambers including the picture gallery, but the southern wing was never finished. In the interior of the propylaea the Ionic order is used. The ceilings were richly decorated with marble beams, coffered, painted and gilded. The masonry is of high quality and the refinements excellent. The approach to the propylaea is very steep and was originally by means of a zig-zag path and ramp, suitable for sacrificial animals in the processions, which led to the central portico; later, this was replaced by steps (**29**).

The Tower of the Winds, Athens c. 40 B.C.

This weather guide and clock was designed by *Andronicus Cyrrus*. It is octagonal and under its cornice has a deep frieze of panels representing personified winds. On the north-east and north-west sides are porticoes with Corinthian columns and on the south side a circular chamber. The roof is of marble blocks originally surmounted by a bronze triton. The Corinthian capitals are interesting designs, having only one row of acanthus leaves, no volutes but a top row of tall, narrow leaves (**26**). This is the only surviving Greek horologium (**40**, PLATE 8).

The Choragic Monument of Lysicrates, Athens, c. 334 B.C.

Erected by *Lysicrates* to commemorate the success of his company in the Choric dances, the monument is a circular pedestal of Pentelic marble standing on a square stone base. Its chief interest is the Corinthian order which is used in the form of six attached half columns surrounding the pedestal. These have very beautiful capitals designed with a lower row of lotus leaves, while above is a row of acanthus leaves and between them eight petalled flowers. The frieze is sculptured and the cornice is crowned with anthemion decoration. The roof, of one block, is slightly convex, ornamented by acanthus foliage and was surmounted by a tall bronze tripod—a replica of Lysicrates' prize at the festival. Although a small monument, almost hidden in modern Athens, it is of architectural importance because of its early use of such a beautiful example of the Corinthian order (**15** and **39**).

Treasuries

These small buildings are found in sanctuaries and were built by each community to house its offerings. Typical is the *Treasury of the Athenians* at *Delphi*, built originally c. 500 B.C. and reconstructed in 1907. It is a simple Doric building with a two-column porch surmounted by a pediment (**54**).

The Greek Agora

The Greek agora, like the Roman forum, was an open air meeting place for the transaction of business. Each town had one or more which comprised market place, business halls and temples. The long stoas were typical features of every agora. These were long colonnaded buildings, generally in two storeys, which contained shops and offices and enabled people to shop or carry out their business protected from sun and rain. In the *Greek Agora* of *Athens*, the *stoa* originally built by *King Attalos II of Pergamon* (159–138 B.C.), has been reconstructed by the American School of Classical Studies as a museum (**37** and **38**).

Plate 7
Tholos, Delphi, Greece, c. 375 B.C., partly restored

Plate 8
The Tower of the Winds, Athens, *c.* 40 B.C.

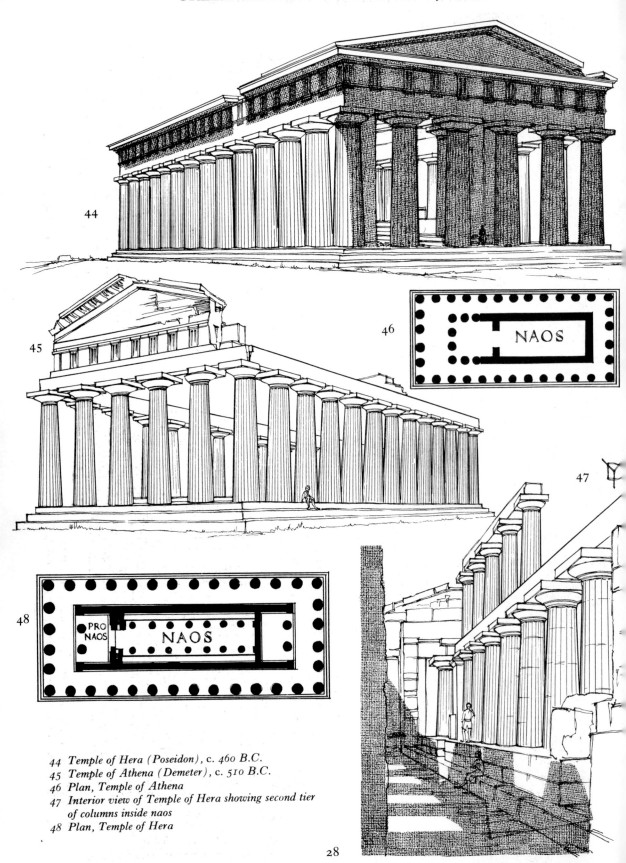

44 *Temple of Hera (Poseidon), c. 460 B.C.*
45 *Temple of Athena (Demeter), c. 510 B.C.*
46 *Plan, Temple of Athena*
47 *Interior view of Temple of Hera showing second tier of columns inside naos*
48 *Plan, Temple of Hera*

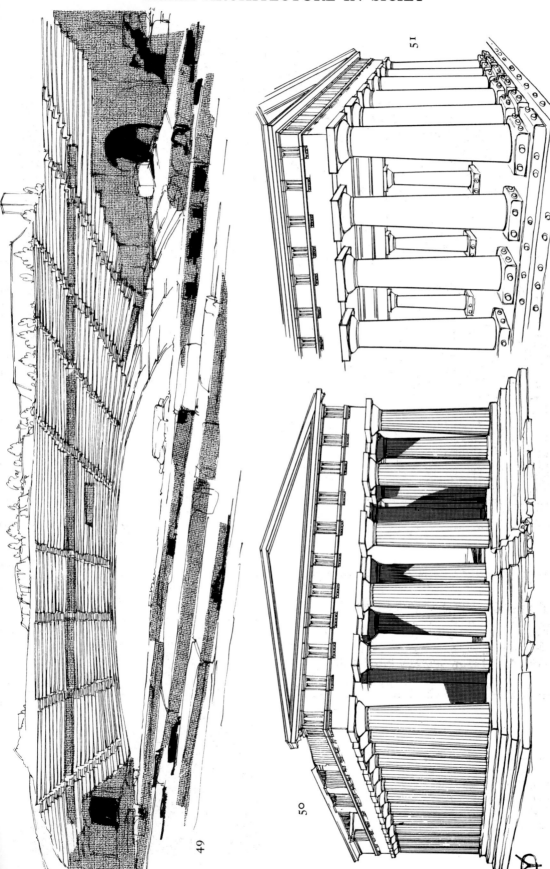

51 *Temple at Segesta, late fifth century B.C.*

49 *The theatre at Syracuse, third to second century B.C.*

50 *The Temple of Concord at Agrigento, late fifth century B.C.*

52 The Theatre and Temple of Apollo, c. 510 B.C.
   (altered later by the Romans)
53 Tholos to Minerva, c. 390 B.C.
54 Treasury of the Athenians, c. 500–480 B.C.

Theatres

The early Greek theatre performance consisted of dancing and chanting which told the story of the drama. The theatre design itself evolved according to these requirements. There was a circular space called the *orchestra*, meaning dancing place, and the *auditorium* was semi-circular in form and hollowed out from a curving hillside. It rose in tiers of seats cut into the rock which were sometimes marble-faced. As the drama developed and actors were introduced, a *stage* (skene) was added to provide entrance and exit accommodation also changing places for the actors (see plan **55**). Nearly all Greek theatres have been altered later by the Romans, who built a larger stage and reduced the circular orchestra to a segment of a circle. One example which retains its original form, though it has been partly restored, is that at *Epidauros*, one of the largest Greek theatres, measuring *c.* 390 feet across the top. It was designed by *Polykleitos the Younger* in *c.* 350 B.C. The acoustics are remarkable, as all visitors to the theatre know who have experimented for themselves. It is in present day use for drama and opera (**55** and **56**). In *Athens* the *Theatre of Dionysos*, built under the acropolis, is a smaller example (**57,** PLATE 12). At *Priene* in Asia Minor survives much of the characteristic Hellenistic theatre form where a raised stage for the actors was built in front of the scene building. The large theatre at Syracuse in *Sicily*, built third to second century B.C. has, like the one at *Taormina* nearby had its orchestra reduced to a semi-circle in later times, as also has the theatre at *Delphi*, built into the lower slopes of Mount Parnassos (**49, 52, 129**).

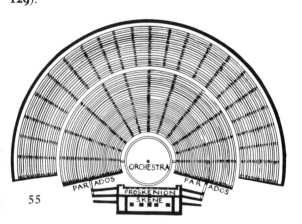

55

55 Typical Greek theatre plan, Epidauros, c. 350 B.C.

The Odeion

These were concert halls, also constructed for open-air performances. There is an interesting example in *Athens* near to the theatre of Dionysos under the acropolis hill. It was built in the fifth century B.C., altered by *Herodes Atticus* in A.D. 161 and has now been restored for present-day performances.

The Stadion

This was a foot race-course later used for general athletic competition. It was usually a stade in length (that is, 600 Greek feet) and was set into the side of a hill to provide seating for spectators. The ground had long straight parallel sides terminating at the far end in a semi-circle and at the starting end in a short straight side. The *stadion in Athens* was originally constructed in 331 B.C. but was rebuilt in marble in 1896 for the first Olympic Games of modern times and accommodates 50,000 spectators. There are several examples in a good state of preservation such as the one at *Delphi*, high up on the mountainside above the theatre (**58**), also at *Epidauros, Rhodes, Miletus, Priene* and *Aphrodisias*.

Domestic Architecture

The remains in this field are scanty, and nothing equivalent to Roman work at Pompei or Ostia has been discovered. The most fruitful sites are on the *island of Delos* and at *Priene* in *Asia Minor*, where the houses are mainly fourth century and later. It appears that the Greek house was one-storeyed, designed with rooms grouped round a courtyard or garden which probably had a peristyle and perhaps porticoes. There were few windows which were small and placed high in the walls. A narrow passage gave access to the street. The house walls had stone bases but above this were of sun dried brick and wood, stuccoed and painted on the interior; roofs were tiled, floors of mosaic. There were living rooms and a bathroom; the latrine was in the court. Each house contained a place for worship with an altar.

Plate 9
Heifers led to sacrifice. South frieze of the Parthenon, Athens *c.* 440 B.C.

Plate 10
North frieze, Parthenon Athens *c.* 447–430 B.C.

Plate 11
Caryatid figure, south
porch, Erechtheion,
Acropolis. Athens *c.*
421 B.C.
Plate 12
Nereid. Nereid
Monument Xanthos
Asia Minor *c.* 370 B.C.

GREEK THEATRES

56 Theatre at Epidauros, designed by Polykleitos the Younger, c. 350 B.C.
57 Theatre of Dionysos, Athens, (below the Acropolis), various building periods, chiefly fifth and fourth centuries

58

*58 The Stadion, Delphi,
(a stade in length
i.e. 600 Greek feet)*

Tombs

Mausoleum of Halicarnassos (Asia Minor)

Probably the most famous of all tombs, this monument was built for Artemisia in memory of her husband King Mausolos (hence mausoleum) after his death in 353 B.C. It was designed by *Pythius* and *Satyros*, but knowledge of its exact form is not definite as the building does not exist and the materials have been re-used. We have accounts from Pliny and Vitruvius, who base their descriptions upon the original designs. A number of conjectural restorations have been made, but these differ in form as well as detail. An interesting example of these is in the British Museum, carried out by Cockerell. Also in the Museum are parts of the sculptured frieze, horses and quadriga and statues of Mausolos and Artemisia. The monument, which was one of the wonders of the ancient world, stood on a square podium, was surrounded by a peristyle and surmounted by a pyramid with quadriga above. The base was about 100 feet square; the order was Ionic; the total height was 136 feet. One of the chief features of Halicarnassos was the sculpture, carried out by four of Greece's outstanding artists—*Bryaxis, Leochares, Timotheus* and *Scopas*.

Just south of Halicarnassos was *Cnidos*, famous for the *Lion Tomb* which was a similar monument but in the Doric order and surmounted by a colossal recumbent lion. Other interesting tombs included the *Harpy Tomb* at *Xanthos c.* 550 B.C. and the *Nereid Tomb*, (see PLATE 12). Sculpture from all these examples is on view at the British Museum.

Ornament and Mouldings

Greek *ornament* was of the highest quality and has never been surpassed in classical architecture. Designers used their decoration sparingly in order to enhance the architectural form. The motifs came from many sources: Egyptian, Assyrian, Minoan and Mycenaean, and were commonly based on natural plant and animal forms; the Greeks did not, however, use these realistically, but conventionalised them. Each moulding and part of the building was assigned its own ornament, all forms of which were characterised by simplicity of line, refinement and symmetry. Colour and gold were used to pick out the enrichments in carved marble. Among the natural motifs common to Greek ornament are the *acanthus leaf* (the spikier, *spinosus* variety) (**19, 26** and **27**), the *anthemion* or honeysuckle (**15, 16,**

59

60

62

63

64

66

67

59 *Flanking doorway column in grey-green limestone. Treasury of Atreus, Mycenae, c. 1330 B.C.*

60 *Frieze above doorway, as above, but in red marble*

61 *Tympanum decoration, as above*

62 *Anthemion ornament, Tholos, Acropolis, Athens, c. A.D. 14*

63 *Anthemion and bead and reel ornament, Delphi, late sixth century*

64 *Typical Minoan decoration, Knossos, c. 1500 B.C.*

65 *North porch doorway, the Erechtheion, Athens, 421–405 B.C.*

66 *Entablature and decoration, Tholos at Epidauros, mid-fourth century*

67 *Anta capital and decoration, east portico of the Erechtheion, Athens*

22, 23, 62, 63, 65, 66 and 67), the *palm*, the *rosette* (65 and 66), the *sphinx* and the *griffin* and *lion's head* (66). *Moulding decoration*, apart from the popular anthemion, included *egg and dart*, i.e. life and death (22, 25 and 67), *leaf and dart* (or tongue) (67), *guilloche*, like a plait (16 and 21), *fret* (66), *bead and reel* (16, 25, 62, 63 and 67), *dentil* (15), and the *scroll* (14, 16, 18, 22, 25, 27, 28, 59, 61, 63, 66 and 67).

Although *classical mouldings* are basically of the same form they vary in their usage and proportion according to country and period. The purpose of mouldings, apart from creating a projecting cornice to throw off the rain, is to define and beautify the lines of a building by means of light and shade. In Greece, where sunlight is brilliant, subtly curved and projecting mouldings are adequate; Roman ones are deeper and coarser while Renaissance examples in France and England are deeper still. In *Greek architecture* they comprise the *cyma recta* and *cyma reversa*, the former generally decorated by anthemion, the latter by leaf and tongue (67); the *ovolo*, with egg and tongue (67); the *fillet*, a flat separating moulding; the *corona* (23), the vertical face of the upper cornice often decorated by fret ornament; the *astragal*, with bead and reel (67); the *cavetto*, a hollow; the *torus*, a larger astragal often with guilloche enrichment (21); the *scotia*, a deeper hollow.

Sculpture

Little original Greek sculpture survives, whether *in situ* on buildings or in museums: the work in museums is predominantly copied or restored and most of that on the buildings is mutilated and any colour has gone. Despite these heavy handicaps the magnificence of the work comes through and makes plain the fact that sculptured decoration to the Greeks was an integral part of architecture. Thus, while their architecture was the finest and purest in classical style, their sculpture has also never been surpassed. It is fortunate that the Romans reproduced so much of the Greek work for it is due to their energies that we owe much of our knowledge of Greek sculpture. Some Roman copies are poor, but many are excellent and possession of these copies is far better than having no record of the originals at all. Much Greek sculpture was architectural in purpose and

design. Figure sculpture was framed by the triglyphs and pediment mouldings. Much of it had religious inspiration and was used to decorate temples in the form of friezes, metopes, pedimental groups and cult statues. Subjects were commonly of two types; to illustrate the daily life of the period and the Greek legends. Life-size portrait sculpture belongs to the middle and later periods. The Greeks used stone, marble and bronze as their chief sculptural materials but most of the surviving work is in stone or marble; the bronze was mostly melted down later. Early bronze work was in plates fastened to a wooden core. Later examples were cast. The Greeks worked also in terracotta, especially for smaller items, possibly influencing later Etruscan work in this medium.

There are *four chief periods* in Greek sculpture: work prior to 450 B.C.; 450–400 B.C.; the fourth century and *c.* 340–146 B.C. *Early sculpture*, that prior to about 650 B.C., was generally of wood on a small scale. Subsequently, contact with Egypt and Assyria led to larger works in stone being attempted by the Greeks. The eastern characteristics in sculptural design are apparent in the Greek works of the seventh century. Figures stand stiffly, one foot slightly in advance of the other, arms at sides elbows slightly bent and heads facing front. The figures are generally nude and anatomical features are stylised. By the early sixth century attempts were made to study anatomy and movement and to fit the figures to the architectural shape, for example, the pediment. Animals, particularly lions and bulls, and sphinxes were used. The *first half of the fifth century* is the early classical period from which a number of architectural examples are available. From the *Temple of Zeus* at *Olympia* 465–457 B.C. are the pedimental sculptures and metopes. The *eastern pediment* has a centrepiece of five figures and a chariot; it illustrates sacrifice to Zeus and is still and forceful. The *western pedimental sculpture* is, in contrast, full of movement and depicts the struggle between Lapiths and Centaurs with a magnificent central figure of Apollo. There are a number of metopes extant, some showing the exploits of Hercules. From the *Treasury of the Athenians* at *Delphi c.* 490 the metopes illustrate the adventures of Hercules and Theseus. From the *Temple of Aphaia* at *Aegina* come pedimental sculptures. All these examples show more vigorous movement and realism than the archaic sculpture, also more naturalistic drapery, and are vivid in design and form.

450–400 B.C.

This was a prosperous time. Under the leadership of *Pericles* art and architecture flourished reaching the zenith of the classical style. The *Parthenon* represents all that is finest in Greek Doric temple building both architecturally and sculpturally. *Pheidias* was in charge of the sculptural decorations of the Parthenon and it is in the remains of this work that we can appreciate the wonderful quality of Greek art of this period and in particular the work of the greatest of Greek sculptors. Pheidias' contemporaries regarded his architectural sculpture as inferior to his great statues such as the colossal figures of *Athena Parthenos* in Athens and of *Zeus* at Olympia. We only possess copies of doubtful authenticity of such works but we can see considerable sections of the Parthenon sculptures—frieze, metopes and pedimental—in the national museums of Athens, Paris, Rome and London. Of the immense quantity of sculpture on the Parthenon, Pheidias carried out some and designed and supervised the remainder. There were over 50 large figures in the pediments, 92 metopes and over 520 feet of continuous frieze all carried out in 15 years. The quality of the work is magnificent,

the drapery is lively and vivid, the horses, the bulls and the men are breathing, pulsing living beings, yet subtle and never overstated. In the frieze especially, the composition is always alive, never monotonous. The handling of the horses and bulls is in low relief yet distinguishing one horse behind another, with the four legs of each animal in recessive perspective giving the appearance of great depth of relief in reserve. The detail is fine and yet the unity of the whole frieze is intact. The subject is the procession of the Panathenaia, a sacred Athenian festival, depicting men and animals moving inexorably and perpetually forward round the building. Large sections of this frieze are now admirably displayed in the British Museum (PLATES 4 and 5). The metopes in high relief are mainly single combat groups between Greeks and Amazons or Centaurs and Lapiths. The part-bull part-man centaurs provide effective contrast to horse and man (PLATE 2).

Pheidias dominates the sculpture of Greece but in his own age there were a number of other fine sculptors. In architectural sculpture there are the famous caryatid figures of the *Erechtheion* south porch *c.* 420 (PLATE 6) (one of which is in the British Museum), the sculptured frieze and pedimental figures from the *Theseion, Athens*, in high relief, the frieze of the *Temple of Athena Nike* on the Athens acropolis *c.* 425 and the frieze from the great altar at *Pergamon* 168 B.C. representing a battle between Gods and Greeks.

Etruscan and Roman: 750 B.C. to A.D. 476
Etruscan Eighth Century B.C. to First Century B.C.

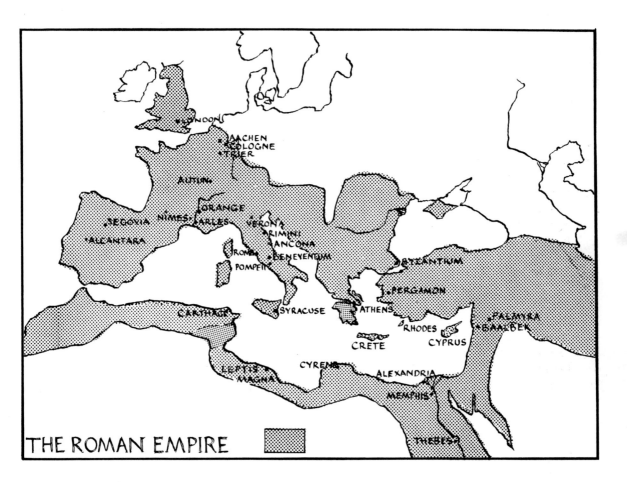

THE ROMAN EMPIRE

Despite archaeological discoveries which are still being made year by year and which throw more light upon the Etruscan civilisation, knowledge of these people, their origins, their way of life is still far from complete. It is generally accepted* that the Etruscans were of foreign origin, of a mixed Hellenic and Oriental culture, probably but far from certainly from Asia Minor, and that they established themselves in central Italy, in the area between the Arno and the Tiber, in the eighth century B.C. The civilisation appears to have developed and grown quickly and exten-

sively and, by about 700 B.C., the Etruscans were living an urban life in fine cities with wealthy citizens, and were capable of a high standard of building and visual and literary arts.

Although so far no one has succeeded in interpreting the Etruscan language we can fully appreciate their sculpture, painting and craftsmanship. No complete buildings are intact, but there are extensive remains in walling, gateways, arches and in tombs. It is in the tombs that so many fine works of art and crafts have been found. Few early peoples, apart from the

In Roman times there was one theory that the Etruscans originated in Italy.

Egyptians, have left to posterity so much workmanship quite undisturbed through the passage of time.

The Etruscans were great builders and in this respect they occupy a similar relationship to the Romans in the development of architecture as do the Pelasgic and Minoan peoples to the Greek. Etruscan builders fully understood the art of building in stone and used huge (cyclopean) blocks, generally without cement. They showed great skill in constructing polygonal block walling and introduced into Europe—though it is questionable that they invented it—vaulting by dressed stones. They constructed in this way true arches with radiating voussoirs, but a controversy exists as to whether the European origins here are Etruscan or Roman, as Etruscan examples all date from the later period of the third century B.C. onwards when Roman supremacy over the Etruscans was being established.*

Etruscan Remains

City Walls, Arches and Gateways

There are numerous hill towns in central Italy where can be seen extant remains of Etruscan city walling. Examples from the sixth century B.C. exist, generally of a cruder type of masonry at, for example, Volterra and Cortona. There are also, dating from about 500 B.C., gateways of the lintel and arched types. A famous lintel example is the *Porta Saracena* at *Segni*, originally part of the city wall, but now about a mile outside the modern town up on the steep hillside. This has a large lintel stone and the sides slope inwards towards the top (69). There is another gateway of this type at nearby *Arpino*, the *Porta dell'Arco*. An early arched gateway is in the town walls of *Ferentino* where the *Porta Sanguinaria* has radiating stone voussoirs; here the sides are vertical (72). A particularly good example is the *town gateway* at *Volterra*, of the third century B.C., which has cyclopean blocks fitted to make vertical sides, and radiating voussoirs which are exceptionally well prepared. The gateway is several feet in thickness but the outer face is in better condition (71).

The two best known Etruscan archways are both of later date: the *Arch of Augustus* at *Perugia* and the *Cloaca Maxima* in *Rome*. The Perugian

The Roman Conquest of Etruria is dated at about 280

arch is called Augustan as the upper part was added by Augustus. The archway itself is in fine condition and dates from the third century B.C. It forms part of the Etruscan walls to the city and is the best extant example of Etruscan masonry. It is built of large blocks of travertine stone and the arch has two concentric rings of radiating voussoirs. Above this is a 'Doric' type frieze with 'Ionic' pilasters in place of triglyphs (73). Also in Perugia is the arch of the *Porta Marzia*, with a similar frieze and Ionic style columns at the sides (70). The *Cloaca Maxima* is a floodwater drain built by the Etruscans in the sixth century B.C. to drain the Forum Romanum. It was for many years claimed to be the earliest example of the true arch in Europe, but it is now recognised that it was constructed in the sixth century as an open drain and that it was only roofed over with its present stone vault of three concentric rings of radiating voussoirs in 184 B.C. Its exit into the Tiber can still be seen in Rome near the Ponte Rotto (68).

Etruscan Temples

Extensive remains of the foundations of such temples make it relatively easy to establish their plan, but reconstruction of the superstructure is more speculative as almost all the walls and trabeation have disappeared. Vitruvius provides a clear description of an example of the late period from which it seems that the temples contained three cells placed side by side and dedicated to three different deities. There was a portico, generally of wood, with posts supporting beams, and decoration was in terracotta. Larger temples generally had one or two rows of columns in front with wide intercolumniation. A smaller example from *Alatri* has been re-erected and restored in the Court of the *Villa Giulia* in *Rome*. It has a two columned portico and, behind this, a central doorway opening into the cella (76).

Etruscan Houses

Very little was known about these from actual remains until recent excavations at S. Giovenale by the Swedish expedition established plans from some foundations there. The layout of a seventh century B.C. example shows a large hall with entrance porch.

Etruscan Tombs

It is from this source that much has been learnt of the style of domestic building, the arrangement and designs of house interiors, of sculpture, painting and craftmanship in terracotta, metal and jewellery. The Etruscans put their burial places outside their cities, and due to the care with which they constructed the tombs many examples have been discovered intact, from the eighteenth century onwards. There are two chief types of tombs which date from the seventh to first century B.C. One type consists of a tumulus, or burial mound, of earth, circular in plan and surrounded at the base by a stone wall. There is a rectangular entrance and inside is the burial chamber(s). The other type is a rectangular tomb cut in the rock, where such rock—generally volcanic tufa—was suitably soft. In these cases the chambers are approached down a flight of steps. Tombs vary greatly in size and elaboration, from a nobleman's tomb with several chambers, richly decorated and furnished by household objects used in life, to simple, single-cell designs for an ordinary family. In the more elaborate tombs can be seen the manner of domestic interior design, for the rock has been hewn to imitate rafters and ridge-piece. Columns and piers of stone support the roof; these have carved capitals, some in voluted 'Ionic' designs (83). Many chambers have characteristic semi-circular headed windows and either semi-circular or square headed door openings with sloping sides (78 and 81). There are often wall recesses holding utensils and objects used in life such as helmets, swords, knives, kitchen pots and pans etc. Stone funerary beds are set on each side of the main chamber.

Two of the principal Etruscan cities which possess such examples in quantity are *Tarquinia* and *Cerveteri*. *Modern Tarquinia* (earlier known as Corneto but now re-named after the Etruscan Tarquinii) is built near to the original city. The enormous necropolis is adjacent and contains hundreds of tombs cut down into the tufa over a distance of two miles. The tombs are rock hewn chambers, many beautifully decorated by wall paintings in rich colours. They are mainly of the fourth, fifth and sixth centuries B.C. and illustrate episodes and customs in Etruscan life. Some of these are in exceptionally good condition.

Cerveteri is built near the extensive necropolis which served the Etruscan city of *Caere*, one of their largest towns, near the sea and only a few miles from Rome. The tombs represent a period of wealth and expansion in the sixth and seventh centuries B.C. Many of the finds in sculpture and decoration have been taken to museums, but the chambers remain. These are of several types but predominantly of the circular tumulus design with its stone base and decorative cornice (80 and 84). Later tombs here have no tumulus above but consist of a single large room cut into the stone. The room is reproduced as a house interior, furnished with benches, pillars, wall paintings and utensils. The larger tumuli are nearly 100 feet in diameter and contain several chambers as a house does rooms. The ceilings are coffered or have sloping beams and are supported by decorative pillars (81 and 83).

Sculpture and Ornament

Much of the extant Etruscan *sculpture* is in the form of sarcophagi in stone and bronze. The Etruscans are particularly noted for their terracotta work, a medium at which they excelled (74, 75, 77 and PLATE 13).

Ornament also was commonly made in terracotta, often in the form of panels and friezes. Here the anthemion is a popular motif (77). *Moulding ornament* includes a version of egg and tongue, anthemion, leaves and flowers. There are several types of *capital*; a version of Ionic as in 82 and 83 and a Doric (or Tuscan) which developed from the early bulbous form (VII) to a more sophisticated version (VIII).

Roman 146 B.C. to A.D. 476

It is traditionally accepted that it was in about the year 753 B.C. that a tribe of people settled near the Tiber on the Palatine Hill. Here they built and established a walled city. They extended their domain and carried out raids upon neighbouring peoples. Until nearly 500 B.C. they were ruled by tribal kings. After this Rome became a republic which steadily expanded and absorbed the adjacent peoples and countryside. Piecemeal the country of Italy became a vassal state to the City of Rome: the Etruscans were absorbed; the Sicilians, Carthage and North Africa were

Plate 13
Etruscan Sarcophagus
from Chiusi, Italy *c.*
150 B.C.
Plate 14
Stucco wall relief,
Tepidarium. Forum
Baths, Pompeii, Italy

Plate 15
Detail, Trajan Column
Rome A.D. 114
Plate 16
Sculptured panel.
Arch of Galerius,
Thessaloniki, Greece

annexed and, in 146 B.C., Greece became a part of Rome. It is from this time onwards that the architectural style of Rome was developed and crystallised.

The expansion of Rome did not, however, cease at this point. In 30 B.C. Egypt was absorbed and campaigns were extended northwards and westwards in Europe, culminating in A.D. 43 with the successful annexation of most of Britain. For 400 years after this the Romans enslaved, organised and civilised the enormous area of their known world, which encircled the Mediterranean and stretched from Spain in the west to the Black Sea in the east, from Britain in the north to Egypt in the south. They first conquered the territories, then brought their rule of law, made roads, built cities and stayed to civilise with their arts, literature and industry. For, unlike conquerors before and after, the Romans did not only take from their subject peoples, they contributed also, and the result of these contributions in road communications, law and administration, heating systems, architecture and art has had a permanent effect in Europe despite the 1000 years which intervened between the collapse of the Western half of the Roman Empire and the rise of the Renaissance.

The republic of Rome was severely shaken in 44 B.C. by the murder of Julius Caesar. There followed a time of uncertainty and bloodshed which was eventually resolved when the republic developed into an empire with Augustus as its first emperor from 27 B.C. The Augustan period from then until his death in A.D. 14 was one of the great and successful ages of man and, architecturally, this is reflected. in the many great buildings which were erected under the auspices of Augustus whose boast was that when he came to Rome it was a city of bricks but that he left it a city of marble. There is a basic truth in his assertion, for before his time the use of marble was rare in Roman architecture. It was from the first century B.C. onwards that the vast white marble quarries at Carrara were developed and that quantities of Greek marble were shipped to Italy from Hymettus and Pentelicus.

A number of the Roman emperors were great patrons of building and endorsed and encouraged extensive schemes of architectural development. Among the most outstanding of these were:

Augustus   27 B.C. to A.D. 14

* This marble was only a veneer covering the brick and concrete buildings.

Tiberius   A.D. 14–37
Nero   A.D. 54–68
Vespasian   A.D. 70–9
Titus   A.D. 79–81
Trajan   A.D. 98–117
Hadrian   A.D. 117–138
Marcus Aurelius   A.D. 161–180
Septimius Severus A.D. 193–211
Caracalla   A.D. 211–17
Diocletian   A.D. 284–305
Maxentius   A.D. 306–12
Constantine   A.D. 312–337

It was in the Imperial age that the full magnificence and display of Roman architecture was reached. Before the first century B.C. little is heard of its quality. It was after the annexation of Greece that Rome began to take the place of the nation that she had absorbed and the civilisation which she had destroyed. But the Romans were never to replace the Greeks as artists. They excelled in and developed the arts of building, of engineering and of town planning. Their schemes, especially under the emperors, were extensive, grandiose, eye-catching, but never of the same meticulous quality of craftmanship and design that the Greeks had attained before them. The Romans did not try to compete in the sculptural and decorative field. They imported artists and artisans from Greece to carry out this work for them and to ornament their buildings; they also imported actual sculpture from Greece for the same purpose. It is, however, due to the large number of copies which the Romans had made of Greek masterpieces, some of them of high quality, that we owe our wide knowledge of such work today.

Extensive building schemes were projected not only in Rome and in Italy but all over the Empire. Wherever Roman civilisation went there were created cities, each with their buildings necessary to Roman life: the central fora, the basilicas, temples, baths, circuses and amphitheatres. The remains of these edifices in Italy, France, Germany, Spain, Yugoslavia, Greece, Rumania and Asia Minor give us a clear idea of their way of life as well as their modes of building and it is a much more complete picture than that which we have from the Greek civilisation because of its very complexity and variety. Greek remains are largely temples; Roman ones represent every facet of Roman life.

ETRUSCAN ARCHES AND GATEWAYS, SIXTH TO THIRD CENTURY

68 The Cloaca Maxima, Rome. Exit into the River Tiber near the Ponte Rotto, sixth century B.C. Roofed over 184 B.C.
69 Porta Saracena, Segni, Town Gateway (now outside the present town)
70 Porta Marzia, Perugia (archway now blocked up)
71 Town Gateway, Volterra, third century B.C.
72 Porta Sanguinaria, Ferentino, Town Gateway
73 Arch of Augustus, Perugia, third century B.C. (only top arch is Augustan)

74 *Antefix, gorgon's head from Capua, terracotta, sixth century B.C.*

75 *Antefix, terracotta, Cerveteri, fifth century B.C.*

76 *Temple from Alatri (restored)*

77 *Terracotta decoration*

78 *Tomb doorway, Cerveteri, sixth century B.C.*

79 *Bronze griffin's head from Chiusi, 650–600 B.C.*

80 *Tumuli, Cerveteri, seventh-fifth century B.C.*

81 *Interior of Tomb of the Funerary Beds, Cerveteri, sixth-fifth century B.C.*

82 *Ionic style capital, Tomb of the Reliefs, Cerveteri, fourth-second century B.C.*

83 *Interior of Tomb of the Capitals, Cerveteri, sixth-fifth century B.C.*

84 *Tumuli, Cerveteri, seventh-fifth century B.C.*

In A.D. 324 Constantine moved his capital to Byzantium and a few years later the Empire was divided into two parts, eastern and western. Early Christian work began to influence the architectural style in the new Christian Roman Empire. In the fifth century Rome was attacked and sacked three times. Finally, in A.D. 476, the western part of the Empire collapsed, and in the eastern part with Byzantium as its capital, architecture developed in a different direction. Of this vast quantity of building which was achieved between 146 B.C. and A.D. 476 only a small fraction exists today and often this is in the best condition in the provinces of the Empire, despite the fact that the examples were generally less magnificent. Such well preserved works can be seen for example in Southern France and Spain, rather than in Italy, and particularly Rome, where greater toll has been taken by the use of marble for rebuilding and by barbarian invasions.

The Roman Architectural Style

The development of the classical style of architecture with trabeated construction belongs to the Greeks, who carried this to the highest possible standard of artistic perfection. The Romans also followed on these lines but adapted the construction to suit their more complex needs. They incorporated the arch and vault into their architectural style, using both lintel and arcuated construction, often in one building. The Greeks had perfected the lintel method of spanning an opening; the Romans adapted the arch from Etruscan designs and from their own development and thus led the way to later variations on this theme. They used the Greek orders, adapted them to their own taste, added two more variations and employed them constructively in temples and basilicas but more often, especially in later work, only decoratively when the arch mode of construction was used, for example, in the Colosseum and the Theatre of Marcellus. The Greeks had built predominantly in only one or two storeys; the Romans built up to four or even five, and the arched type of construction was more suitable for this type of work.

Roman workmanship is often criticised in comparison with Greek for its clumsy detail, as in capitals and mouldings, and for its less subtle proportions of columns and entablature. The Romans appreciated fine art but lacked the artistic sense of the Greeks. They never reached the standard of work evidenced by the Parthenon or the Erechtheion. Their outstanding abilities lay elsewhere and it is to their fine engineering achievements in vaulting such constructions as the Basilica of Constantine and the Baths of Diocletian, or in the building of amphi-theatres such as the Colosseum, or in layouts like the Palace of Diocletian in Split or the Villa of Hadrian at Tivoli that we can appreciate their genius for architectural effect and scale in planning.

Town Planning

Roman cities were planned as far as possible symmetrically on a grid system, although in the case of existing towns which they took over, or of hill sites, geographical problems made this difficult. The city would be encircled by its defensive walls pierced by town gates. The town was laid out in a military camp plan with a wide, straight road crossing the city centre from one side of the town to the other and similar roads intersecting the first at right angles. The town gates were set in the walls where these principal thoroughfares made their exit. The main forum was generally placed at the central cross-roads and round it were grouped the chief buildings of the town. The smaller streets criss-crossed on a grid pattern and the town walls surrounded an eight-sided city. This was considered to be the ideal layout and was followed where a new city was planned. Remains showing this design can be seen in a number of towns, especially where the city has since declined in importance and later building has not obscured the pattern.

Our chief source of information on Roman architecture for the first century B.C. is Marcus Vitruvius Pollio who wrote his famous work *De Architectura*, which he dedicated to Augustus, in 25 B.C. Vitruvius, as we call him, sets out his plans for an ideal Roman city in the first volume of his work.

The Roman Forum

In Roman life the forum corresponded to the Greek agora. It was a large open space surrounded by buildings and provided a meeting place and a centre for commerce and public life. Every town had a forum and large cities more than one. Under the republic the forum was both a market place surrounded by shops and a public meeting place. Under the empire, in large towns, the shops were cleared and it became the site for more magnificent buildings devoted to the administration of justice, bureaucracy and commerce, as well as for worship. There were many temples, set at different angles, not orientated like the Greek ones. The forum was planned symmetrically and was surrounded by covered colonnades to provide shelter from sun and rain.

Rome

At one period there were 17 fora in Rome. The largest of these was the *Forum of Trajan* but the oldest is the *Forum Romanum*, or as it is often called, simply 'the Forum'. Under Imperial rule, a number of emperors added their own forum bearing their name; one forum was not large enough for the needs of the whole city. Since Rome has been continuously inhabited ever since, and as Medieval, Renaissance and Modern cities have been built on the same site, very little is left of any of these fora except the excavated site and fragments of buildings.

The *Forum Romanum* owes its present layout largely to Julius Caesar, who replanned much of it. Originally the forum was a business centre and market place for the inhabitants of the three surrounding hills—Palatine, Capitoline and Esquiline. The great drain, the Cloaca Maxima crosses the valley from north to south and, after its construction in the sixth century B.C. the forum life began. By the second century B.C. it had become a large square surrounded by imposing buildings. A number of reconstructions were made from time to time, especially under Julius Caesar and Augustus. The body of Julius Caesar was burned near the Via Sacra and Augustus had built on the spot the Temple of Divi Julii to his memory. In the time of Augustus also were erected the Temples of Concord, of Castor and Pollux, and the Basilica Julia. The great Basilica of Constantine (Maxentius) was constructed along the Via Sacra in the time of these two emperors.

In the fifth century many buildings were destroyed in the Goth and Vandal invasions and,

later, Christians built churches in the temple ruins. Earthquakes assisted the destruction and the land silted up so that by the Middle Ages only the capitals of the columns stood above ground and the forum's name (Campo Vaccino) reflected its purpose—grazing land for cattle. A plan of the Forum Romanum as it is today is shown in Fig. **86** while a reconstruction of it as it was under Imperial Rome, looking towards Capitol Hill, is illustrated in Fig. **85**.

Building Materials and Construction

Unlike the Greeks, whose building materials were principally limited to marbles, the Romans were fortunate in the availability of a wide variety of materials in Italy itself. Much of their building was in brick and concrete faced, in republican times, chiefly with stucco and, under the empire, with marble. A useful selection of *stone* was also to hand; travertine, a form of hard limestone from the area near Tivoli, also tufa and peperino, both of volcanic origin. These were all used in large blocks for strong walling and arch voussoirs. *Bricks* were of two types, sun dried and kiln burnt, and these were widely employed, particularly in provincial work. The bricks were laid in alternate courses with stone or concrete, or were used only as a facing on a concrete core. They were about an inch to one and a half inches in thickness and nearly two feet square. The mortar joints between bricks were thick, generally about the same as the bricks themselves. The material which more than any other influenced the whole course and design of Roman architecture was *concrete* and this made the vaulting of huge spans possible. The exceptional strength and durability of Roman concrete was due to the substance *pozzolana*, a volcanic ash, found in quantity in the volcanic areas near Rome and Naples and named after the village of Pozzuoli where the best quality supplies were available. *Pozzolana* when mixed with the excellent lime from the local limestones formed an extremely hard concrete, to which base was also added brick and travertine fragments to provide a solid core for walling and vaulting. The concrete was poured between boards to make walls and over centering for arches and vaults.

Marble was not in general use in Rome until

the early days of the Empire. It was retained chiefly for decoration and facings to walls, floors and vaults. Marbles were imported from all over the Empire, particularly from Hymettus and Pentelicus in Greece, while Italian quarries were developed to provide, in particular, Carrara, Cipollino and Pavonazzo marbles. Granite and alabaster were also imported with precious materials such as porphyry to give richness and lustre to interiors. Roman columns were generally monolithic and unfluted. This method was more suited to hard materials like granite and cipollino marble and shows the veining to advantage. Despite the enormous quantities of marble used on buildings in Imperial Rome, little remains today as it was nearly all used in later ages for further building and decoration.

Metals such as bronze were generally retained for decorative use only and for sculpture, although there are individual examples of constructional needs, as at the Pantheon where the roof tiles and ceiling panels were of bronze.

For buildings which were not faced with marble or made of ashlar blocks, a marble *stucco* generally covered the brick and concrete walling. This material was most durable and the powdered marble imparted a brilliance to the finished surface. The stucco was applied in several coats to a thickness of up to three inches. Such work gave excellent protection to the wall surface. Much thinner coating was given to columns, capitals and other decorative features.

Methods of Construction

In Greek trabeated architecture the length of the lintel had determined the intercolumniation. As the Romans turned more and more towards arcuated construction, with the orders used in a decorative capacity there was no such restriction and the columns are sometimes separated by a distance as great as their height. In the buildings with a number of storeys they frequently used a different order on each storey, whilst the columns were lined up one above the other and the entablatures acted as string courses. The Colosseum shows the fine architectural effect which such a system can provide (**121**). In these circumstances the columns are placed on pedestals instead of just bases—a further breakaway from Greek tradition. Another instance of

this is seen in later examples of Imperial building where the entablature is continued round the arch or where free-standing columns (generally in interiors) possess their own entablature, often surmounted by a sculptured figure.

The Arch and Vault

In republican times and for smaller temples and basilicas the Romans followed Greek practice and roofed with timber covering. With the development of Imperial architecture and the need for large public gatherings in baths and basilicas the space was more often vaulted with brick and concrete. It is in this method of construction that the Romans made one of their greatest contributions to architectural development; their work was further adapted and continued in Byzantine and Medieval times. The supporting arches were made of brick and concrete or, more commonly, of stone. The supporting piers were massive, few in number in order not to obscure the interior vista but great in diameter and made into important features of the design. They were faced with beautifully patterned marbles in rich colours. The actual vaults were nearly always of concrete and it was the strength of Roman concrete which made it possible to cover the enormous spaces in this way. Many Roman vault spans were far greater than Gothic ones and were not equalled until the development of steel construction in the nineteenth century. This concrete provided a rigid mass covering the open space. There was, unlike Medieval stone vaults, no lateral thrust and this made possible great vaults such as the Pantheon dome, the largest example in the world. Indeed the tenacity of Roman concrete and mortar was so great that today, in the ruined buildings of the Empire, it can be seen that it is the stone which has fractured not the material which binds it. Some vaults were made with brick ribs and concrete filling while, towards the later days of the Empire, stone vaults were constructed, particularly in the provinces, as at Nîmes and in Syria. In design the vault was either barrel or groined. The barrel vault of semi-circular section was used for smaller buildings and was generally divided into rectangular compartments, with brick construction supported on wood centering and then filled in with concrete. For larger edifices the intersecting or

THE FORUM ROMANUM, ROME

85 *Forum Romanum (reconstruction) looking towards Capitol Hill*
 1) Tabularium   2) Temple of Concord   3) Temple of Vespasian   4) Curia   5) Arch of Septimius Severus
 6) Temple of Saturn   7) Imperial Rostra   8) Arch of Tiberius   9) Column of Phocas   10) Honorary Columns
 11) Basilica Julia   12) Basilica Aemilia   13) Temple of Divus Julius   14) Arch of Augustus   15) Temple of
 Castor   16) Temple of Vesta   17) House of Vestal Virgins   18) Temple of Antoninus and Faustina   19) Temple
 of Romulus   20) Basilica of Constantine   21) To Colosseum   22) Arch of Titus   23) To Palatine Hill   24) To
 Capitol   25) To Temple of Jupiter   26) To Temple of Juno

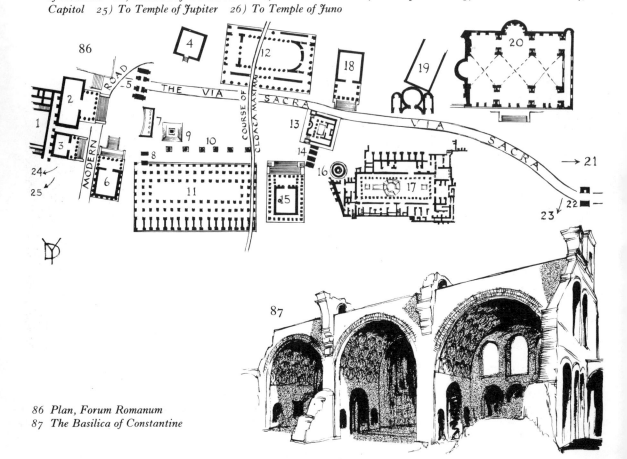

86 *Plan, Forum Romanum*
87 *The Basilica of Constantine*

ROMAN ORDERS AND DETAIL IN ITALY

88 *Triumphal column to Marcus Aurelius, Rome,*
    A.D. 174–80

89 *Corinthian Capital and Entablature, Forum Baths,*
    Ostia, second-fourth century A.D.

90 *The Ionic Order, Temple of Fortuna Virilis, Rome,*
    first century B.C.

91 *The Doric Order, The Colosseum, Rome, A.D. 70–82*

92 *Ionic capital, Forum Basilica, Pompei, first*
    century A.D.

93 *Corinthian entablature, Forum, Pompei*

94 *Corinthian capital, Temple of Minerva, Assisi, first*
    century B.C.

95 *The Corinthian Order, Temple of Castor and Pollux, Rome, A.D. 6*

96 *The Tuscan Order, (reconstruction after Sir William Chambers)*

97 *The Composite Order, The Arch of Titus, Rome, A.D. 81*

98 *The Doric Order, The Baths of Diocletian, Rome, A.D. 290–300*

99 *Base, The Pantheon, Rome, A.D. 120*

100 *Capital, the Pantheon*

101 *Base and Pedestal, the Trajan Column, Rome, A.D. 114*

groined vault, which consists of two barrel vaults meeting one another at right angles, was used. If a long hall was to be vaulted by a cross or groined vault the room would be divided by piers into square bays each of which would be covered by a cross vault. Windows could then be inserted into the upper part of the walls. The Romans used the *dome* construction to a limited extent, but it was left to Byzantium to develop this type of covering to its logical conclusion. In Roman hemispherical domes, brick radiating ribs started at the springing and met at the apex. Semi-circular recesses were covered by half-domes. The interior surface of the vault was covered and decorated in various ways: by stucco, marble or stone facing, by mosaic or by paintings on the plain stucco. A characteristic Roman method was *coffering* such ceilings. The idea was suggested by the pattern made by timber roofed ceilings. The sunken panels or coffers used by the Romans as decoration were formed between the brick ribs or cut into the solid concrete. They were carved decoratively, painted and gilded (**87, 108, 123** and **150**).

The Orders

The Romans used the three Greek orders and developed two more of their own in addition. The proportions differed from the Greek prototypes, the mouldings and carved decoration were less subtle and, generally, more ornate. This is emphasised by the fact that the Doric was the favourite order of the Greeks and was used above all others for important buildings; to the Romans the Corinthian had a greater appeal. Vitruvius gives us a clear account of four of the Roman orders but, having lived in the days of Augustus, he was unable to describe the Composite Order.

Doric

The Roman Doric Order is less massive than the Greek but also less refined. It is often unfluted and, being slenderer, is given a base. The metopes which beautify the Greek frieze are frequently replaced in Roman work by bulls' skulls or garlands. The capital is much less subtle; the Greek echinus becomes a quarter round moulding and the three fillets replace the Greek necking mouldings. Among the best

examples are the Colosseum and the Baths of Diocletian, both in Rome (**91, 98** and **121**).

Tuscan

This is a simplified version of Roman Doric and is generally without flutes or any ornamented mouldings. No clear ancient examples exist, but the order was revived in Renaissance work with the assistance of Vitruvius' *De Architectura*, for example in the colonnade by Bernini in front of S. Peter's Basilica in Rome (**96**).

Ionic

This is the order which bears a closer resemblance to its Greek prototype than any other. Flutes are optional and in the capital angle volutes are often turned in order to present faces to both elevations. The mouldings are more richly decorated than in Greek examples. Among the best Roman versions extant are the Temple of Fortuna Virilis, the Temple of Saturn and the Theatre of Marcellus, all in Rome (**90, 119** and **127**).

Corinthian

One of the reasons for the popularity of this order with the Romans was that, since all four faces of the capital are alike, it presented an interesting view from different angles for the decoration of public buildings and triumphal arches. The shaft was fluted or left plain but the capital bell was strongly delineated, richly decorated and used the softer acanthus leaf design. In later examples all mouldings were enriched, thus somewhat defeating the purpose of the designers for there were no plain members to offset the decoration. Among the many examples, the Temple of Castor and Pollux, the Temple of Mars Ultor and the Pantheon, all in Rome, are very fine (**93, 94, 95, 99, 100, 102, 115, 123** and **124**).

Composite

This order, as its name suggests, was developed as a richer example than the Corinthian, but it is only in the capital that it differs materially. Here, the volutes are larger as in the Ionic order and the upper row of acanthus leaves is replaced by the egg and tongue and bead and reel mouldings

ROMAN ARCHITECTURAL DETAILS FIRST CENTURY B.C. TO FOURTH CENTURY A.D.

102 *Corinthian capital and entablature, Maison Carrée, Nîmes, c. 16 B.C.*

103 *Walling at Ostia*, opus reticulatum *with brick, second century A.D.*

104 *Doorway, Temple of Romulus, Forum Romanum, Corinthian order, bronze doors, A.D. 307*

105 *Stucco wall decoration, tepidarium, Forum baths, Pompei, first century A.D.*

106 *Main doorway, the Pantheon, Rome, A.D. 120*

107 *Entablature, Forum, Ostia*

108 *Coffered vault, Basilica of Constantine, early fourth century A.D.*

109 *Decorated panel, Arch of Tiberius, Orange, c. 30 B.C.*

110 *Scroll decoration, Forum of Trajan, Rome*

from the Ionic capital. The Composite Order was employed particularly on triumphal arches and its use on the Arch of Titus in A.D. 81 is the first recorded instance of its appearance (**97** and **157**).

Interior Decoration

Under the Empire interiors were rich and splendid. Floors were patterned in coloured mosaic and marble. Walls and ceilings were marble faced or decorated with paintings in fresco, tempera or caustic medium. Subjects included figure compositions or landscapes with architectural features introduced. A number of examples are extant at Pompeii or have been removed to the Naples Museum. Sometimes the schemes lacked refinement but rarely richness, colour or magnificence.

Ornament

Roman ornament is a continuation of development from Greek and Etruscan work; it has solidity of mass and grouping, it is bold and vigorous, magnificent, but often lacks the Greek standard of refinement. Similar motifs were used, in particular the acanthus foliage, scrolls and anthemion. The Roman version of the *acanthus leaf* was usually based on the more rounded *acanthus mollis* plant rather than the Greek *acanthus spinosis*, which was spikier and more delicate. The Romans frequently used acanthus foliage in scroll decoration where spiral lines were clothed and decorated by foliage and sheaths with terminal rosettes. They also designed panels and borders with arabesques, mythological forms such as the chimera and griffin, as well as birds, animals and cupids. *Coffered ceilings* were panelled in square, hexagonal or octagonal coffers which had sunken borders enriched with egg and dart or water leaf mouldings and had a central rosette. In capitals, panels and friezes other foliage was also employed: water leaves, ivy, the vine or the olive leaf. All the Greek forms of *moulding enrichment* were used but in less refined form. Examples are illustrated in Figs. **89, 90, 93, 94, 95, 97, 98, 100, 101, 102, 105, 107, 108, 109** and **110**.

Sculpture

Roman work in this field was not original but based on the Greek. The Romans imported a great quantity of sculpture—figures, groups and relief work—from Greece and Etruria and used it to decorate their buildings and homes. They appreciated realism and developed a style of figure sculpture clothed in the toga and also in the cuirass, which is effective and particularly Roman. A great number of equestrian statues must have existed but there are scanty remains of these. One outstanding exception is that of Marcus Aurelius now adorning the centre of Michelangelo's Piazza Campidoglio on Capitol Hill in Rome (volume 2). This is the only example portraying a Roman Emperor which has survived intact from such an early age. Likewise the chariots and horses have disappeared from the triumphal arches, but good quality work exists here in the relief panels, especially in the Arch of Titus and, in another form, on the Trajan Column (PLATES 14, 15, 16, 17, 18, and 19).

Buildings and Extant Remains

Basilicas

The Roman basilica was a hall of justice and a centre for commercial exchange. It was one of the most important of Roman buildings and wherever the Romans built a city the basilica would occupy a central position in or near the forum. The building was rectangular, generally twice as long as wide and had an apse at one or both ends. There were two chief designs. One type had a timber roof which was supported on two rows of columns which divided the hall into a larger, central area and two narrower, side aisles. Later and larger basilicas were roofed with concrete vaults which rested on a few, very large piers. The *Basilica of Trajan*, A.D. 98–112. in *Rome*, designed by Apollodorus of Damascus, was an example of the first type. The central space or nave was 280 feet long and 80 feet wide and the roof was supported on 96 granite columns. Of the basilica, which adjoined the Trajan Forum, there are only scanty remains, as there are of the enormous *Basilica Julia* in the Forum Romanum. The most famous basilica in Rome is the *Basilica of Constantine*, or Maxentius, as it is often called. The Emperor Maxentius began the basilica in A.D. 308 and the work was completed

Plate 17
Arch of Titus, Rome A.D. 81. Panel representing
the Emperor in Triumphal car
Plate 18
Carved marble mask. Theatre, Ostia, Italy
Plate 19
Carved figure supporting seats. The Theatre, Pompeii, Italy

Plate 20
Floor mosaic, Piazzale delle Corporazioni, Ostia,
Italy
Plate 21
Peristyle capital, Palace of Diocletian, Split,
Yugoslavia, *c.* A.D. 300
This is the type of capital that Robert Adam
used extensively in his designs.

Plate 22
Detail, mosaic pavement. Aquileia Cathedral,
Italy, *c.* A.D. 320

by Constantine. It was one of the most imposing structures of the Roman world and its ruins, bordering the Forum Romanum, inspired Michelangelo in his designs for S. Peter's. Four massive, concrete piers, each 14 feet in diameter, supported a vaulted roof. The present remains comprise all one side of the basilica and part of the principal apse on the shorter side. In front of the main piers stood eight gigantic, marble columns, the last of which was removed by Pope Paul V and placed in front of the Church of Santa Maria Maggiore. There was originally a colossal statue of Constantine in the main apse, fragments of which are now in the courtyard of the Conservatori Palace. The basilica was badly damaged in the ninth century earthquake, and in Medieval days it was used, like the Colosseum, as a quarry for building. Due only to its immense solidity are the remains so adequate today. The coffered vault can plainly be discerned and some of the original stucco decoration is adhering to the deep, octagonal coffers (**86, 87, 108** and **XII**).

Temples

Roman designs are based upon the Greek and, more than any other Roman building, temples resemble the Greek prototype. The temple was built to house the deity, but the cella of a Roman temple was much larger than in Greek examples in order to accommodate the sculpture and treasures brought from Greece. Thus the Roman plan for rectangular temples was generally pseudo-peripteral, wherein the cella was widened at the expense of the peristyle, and often the side ambulatory disappeared and half columns attached to the cella walls lined up with those of the front portico; an imposing example of this design is the Maison Carrée at Nîmes (**113**). Circular temples were also built of which the Pantheon is the best known representative (**122–124**). Another feature of Roman temples was that they were generally raised on a podium instead of the Greek stylobate. The Romans considered the front aspect to be the important one and on this elevation the temple was approached by a flight of steps, more on Etruscan lines than Greek. On each side of the steps was a low wall decorated by sculptured figures. Most Roman temples are in the Corinthian order, a few Ionic but rarely Doric.

Rectangular Temples in Rome

There are remains of a number of these in the *Forum Romanum*. In a fragmentary condition, with three columns each, are the *Temple of Castor and Pollux* and the *Temple of Vespasian*. The former has Corinthian capitals, still beautiful despite their mutilation. The central volutes intertwine and a tendril and foliage breaks the line of the abacus between these and the angle volutes. The columns were part of an octastyle portico, each 48 feet high and standing on a 22 feet podium. The entablature has a small, plain frieze but a richly decorated architrave and cornice (**95** and **115**). The Temple of Vespasian (A.D. 94) stands near the *Temple of Concord* and both are now divided from the rest of the Forum by a modern main road.

The *Temple of Saturn* was an early building but was reconstructed in the 4th century A.D. It was large, on a lofty podium, and was fronted by a six-columned Ionic portico in grey granite. Its vaults housed the public treasury.

Two temples owe their better survival to later adaptation into Christian churches. The *Temple of Antoninus and Faustina* (A.D. 142) became the Church of S. Lorenzo in 1602 (**116** and **117**). Its portico of six Corinthian columns exists, as does the finely sculptured frieze of its entablature. Next door to it is the Church of SS. Cosmo and Damiano built in A.D. c. 307 as the *Temple of Romulus*. A miraculous survival here are the wonderful bronze doors still intact within the Roman doorway (**104**).

In the *Forum Boarium*, near the Tiber, survives almost intact the *Temple of Fortuna Virilis*. This remarkable example has been a source of inspiration for architects in Europe since the sixteenth century. The entrance hall at Holkham Hall in England is based upon it. It is a tetrastyle design, built in stone which was originally stucco-covered. It has a fine Ionic portico (**90, 118** and **119**).

The *Forum of Augustus* boasts the remains of the *Temple of Mars Ultor*, a Corinthian temple built in 2 B.C. by Augustus. It was a richly decorated example and still contains a coffered marble ceiling and part of the cella wall.

ROMAN TEMPLES

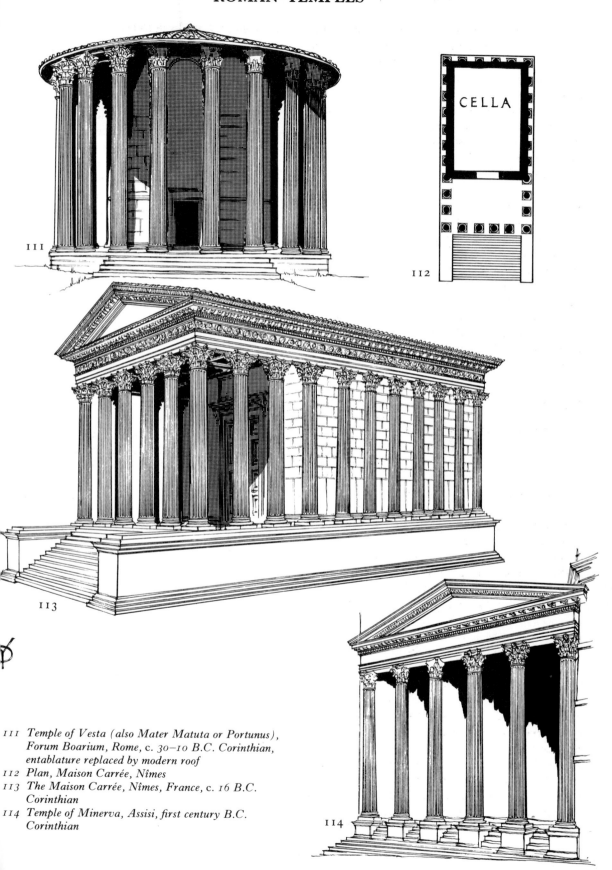

CELLA

111 Temple of Vesta (also Mater Matuta or Portunus),
 Forum Boarium, Rome, c. 30–10 B.C. Corinthian,
 entablature replaced by modern roof
112 Plan, Maison Carrée, Nîmes
113 The Maison Carrée, Nîmes, France, c. 16 B.C.
 Corinthian
114 Temple of Minerva, Assisi, first century B.C.
 Corinthian

DIVO · ANTONINO · ET
DIVAE · FAUSTINAE · EX · SC.

CELLA

CELLA

115 *Temple of Castor and Pollux, Forum Romanum, Rome, Corinthian, A.D. 6 (capitals restored)*
116 *Plan and* 117 *General view of Temple of Antoninus and Faustina (capitals restored), Forum Romanum, Rome, Corinthian, A.D. 142 (interior is church of S. Lorenzo)*
118 *Plan and* 119 *General view of Temple of Fortuna Virilis, Forum Boarium, Rome, Ionic, 100–40 B.C.*
120 *Temple, Forum of Augustus, Rome, Corinthian, 27–14 B.C.*

Circular Temples in Rome

The Pantheon A.D. 120

This is the most famous of all ancient circular temples and, first as a temple, and later as a church, has been in continuous use since its building. It is a remarkable structure and a building of great beauty particularly in the interior. The inscription on the frieze of the portico—'M. AGRIPPA. L.F. COS TERTIUM, FECIT' (Marcus Agrippa, Son of Lucius, consul for the third time, built this)—for many years gave rise to misconceptions regarding the period of building of the Pantheon. For a long time it was felt that Agrippa was the builder, and later that his portico had been re-erected in the later building. Agrippa was the son-in-law of Augustus and an eminent town planner. In 27–25 B.C. he built a temple and baths on the site and called the temple the Pantheon, from the Greek word meaning 'to all the Gods'. Remains of these baths still exist on the south side of the Pantheon. In A.D. 120 the Emperor Hadrian rebuilt both temple and baths and, on the frieze of his new Pantheon, had repeated the original inscription. It was in 1892 that the French architect Georges Chedanne, when making examinations and excavations, discovered bricks, both below and above ground, dated A.D. 125 and 123. It was eventually decided that c. 120 onwards was the correct period of building and that the whole edifice was of one time although there were later restorations by both Septimius Severus and Caracalla, who added their inscriptions on the architrave of the portico below that of Agrippa.

The Pantheon is an unusual temple design. Here the principal emphasis is not on the exterior and the colonnade but on the cella, the interior. As a building it is composed of two parts: the portico and the circular cella. The Emperor Hadrian, who was a great lover of the arts and of Greek architecture in particular, supervised the work himself. Possibly due to his lack of professional knowledge, the exterior marriage of portico and cella is awkward. The porch itself consists of 16 monolithic columns, eight of which, across the front, are of grey Egyptian granite, and the rear columns, internally, are of red granite. The order is Corinthian and the capitals and bases are of white Pentelic marble. The en-tablature and cornice are decorated in a restrained manner and originally the tympanum was ornamented with a bronze relief of Zeus striking down the Greeks. Inside the portico is a well-proportioned doorway, 40 feet high and 20 feet wide, with two bronze-covered doors, each $26\frac{1}{2}$ feet high, between two bronze pilasters. The doors, which are the finest ancient examples in Rome, were originally gold plated. Above the doors is a bronze, openwork screen (**99, 100, 106** and **124**).

The interior of the circular cella is a masterpiece of construction and lighting effect. It is harmoniously balanced in form and mass. The dome, which is the largest ever built* has a diameter of just over 142 feet and is coffered in five concentric rings meeting in the centre in a large circular, unglazed oculus (142 feet from the floor) which is nearly 30 feet across and which is the only, but adequate, source of daylight for the temple. The construction of this dome was an outstanding feat. The material was poured on to hemispherical centering in which the coffered panels had been inserted. The dome diminishes in thickness from nearly 20 feet at the springing to almost 5 feet at the crown and it is built up in horizontal layers of brickwork and concrete where the cement mixture is varied so that the specific gravity diminishes with increasing height. The remainder of the construction is no less remarkable. Half the internal height is wall and half is dome. The walls give the appearance of inclining inwards from floor level. Relieving arches are incorporated into the walls to reinforce them and concentrate the load on to the eight massive piers. These arches are visible on the exterior wall surfaces. The marble floor is slightly convex (**122** and **123**). The Pantheon has survived many vicissitudes; first the barbarian invasions and later the despoliation by the Catholic Church. In A.D. 609 the temple was re-dedicated as a Christian Church to the Madonna and All Martyrs. It was venerated by succeeding Popes but had unfortunately been despoiled, first by the Byzantine Emperor Constans II who, in 655 removed the gilded bronze plates which covered the dome and replaced them with lead and later, in 1625, by the Barberini Pope Urban VIII who destroyed the portico roof in order to use the bronze beams supporting it for his own building schemes. This gave rise to the saying *'quod non fecerunt barbari, fecerunt Barberini'*.

*Comparative domes: S. Peter's Rome 140 feet, Florence Cathedral $137\frac{1}{2}$ feet.

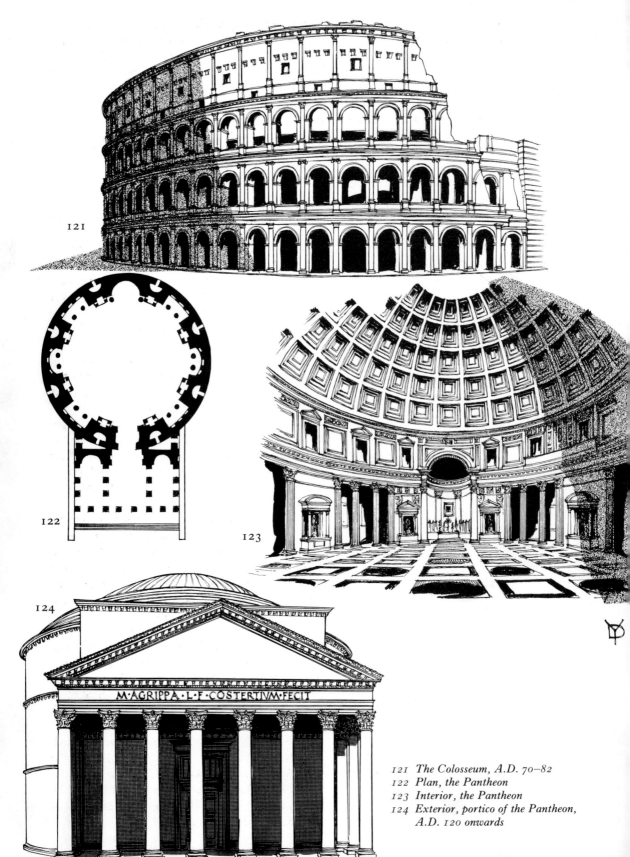

M·AGRIPPA·L·F·COSTERTIVM·FECIT

121 *The Colosseum, A.D. 70–82*
122 *Plan, the Pantheon*
123 *Interior, the Pantheon*
124 *Exterior, portico of the Pantheon,*
   A.D. 120 onwards

During the Renaissance and in later times the Pantheon has aroused the admiration of artists of all nations. Many were inspired by it, for example Raphael and Palladio, and the former is among the many famous men buried there.

The *Temple of Vesta* in the *Forum Romanum* was built in A.D. 205 as the sacred shrine in the city. There is little left of the circular cella which was surrounded by 18 Corinthian columns each $17\frac{1}{2}$ feet high.

More complete is the *Temple of Vesta* in the *Forum Boarium* (also known as Mater Matuta and as Portunus). Also in the Corinthian Order, it has an almost intact peristyle of 20 columns but the entablature has been replaced by a modern roof. The temple has a circular stylobate of marble steps and the columns of Parian marble are $34\frac{1}{2}$ feet high. The cella inside has a diameter of 28 feet. The temple, which was built *c.* 30 B.C. is Greek in the character of its capitals and columns; it is an outstanding example of the circular design (**111**).

Temples in Italy outside Rome

The *Temple of Minerva, Assisi*, was built about 40 B.C. There is a six columned portico raised on a podium. The Corinthian capitals are of Graeco-Roman design. The whole building is simple but effective (**94** and **114**).

At *Tivoli* are the remains of a number of temples, among which are the *Temple of Vesta c.* 27 B.C., Corinthian in design and the *Temple of the Sybils* of the first century B.C. The latter has a circular cella and a peristyle of 18 columns, 24 feet high.

The *Temple of Vespasian* at *Brescia* is a triple-celled example on the Etruscan pattern. It has an entrance portico of 16 columns with projecting porch.

Temples outside Italy

The most important of such examples is also the most complete of all Roman rectangular temples, that now called the *Maison Carrée* at *Nîmes* in *France*. It was built about 16 B.C. and the fact that this area had once been a Greek colony probably accounts for its exceptionally fine detail and proportions. It is raised on a podium

12 feet high, approached by steps on the entrance façade. The order is Corinthian and the design pseudo-peripteral hexastyle. The well proportioned portico is three columns deep and shows Greek influence in its simplicity but the plan, with engaged columns on the sides of the cella, is indisputably Roman (**102**, **112** and **113**). At *Split* in *Yugoslavia* there are the remains of two temples inside the Palace of Diocletian (see pp. 73–5).

The Roman Baths (Roman name thermae from Greek thermos = hot)

These were an institution which was an integral part of life in the days of the Roman Empire. Living conditions at home for those who were not well-to-do lacked space and comfort and the public baths provided free, or at least very cheaply, the daily means for the population to relax, chat, carry out business or social affairs, bathe, receive massage and medical treatment, eat and drink and take part in athletic sports and entertainment. In Imperial Rome alone, there are estimated to have been over 800 thermae of different sizes and accommodation. In the larger establishments there were restaurants, theatre, gardens and fountains, a sports stadium, rest rooms and large halls where poets and philosophers exchanged views and authors gave lectures or read their latest works.

In the bathing establishment itself the operation was long and often complicated. The bather began the process in the hot room (the caldarium); these were small compartments with hot water baths. He then received a rubbing down treatment which included scraping with a strigil. Afterwards he plunged into a cold water swimming bath (the frigidarium) and was then massaged and oiled. The baths provided warm rooms in winter, as in the large, moderately heated room (the tepidarium), and cool, shady gardens in summer, where strollers could walk or sit and relax under the roofed peristyles which surrounded the open courts.

The heating system was by hypocaust in which hot air from furnaces under the building was passed through hollow tiles and bricks in the walls and floor. The temperature could be regulated very exactly for the different needs of caldarium and tepidarium.

ROMAN THEATRES

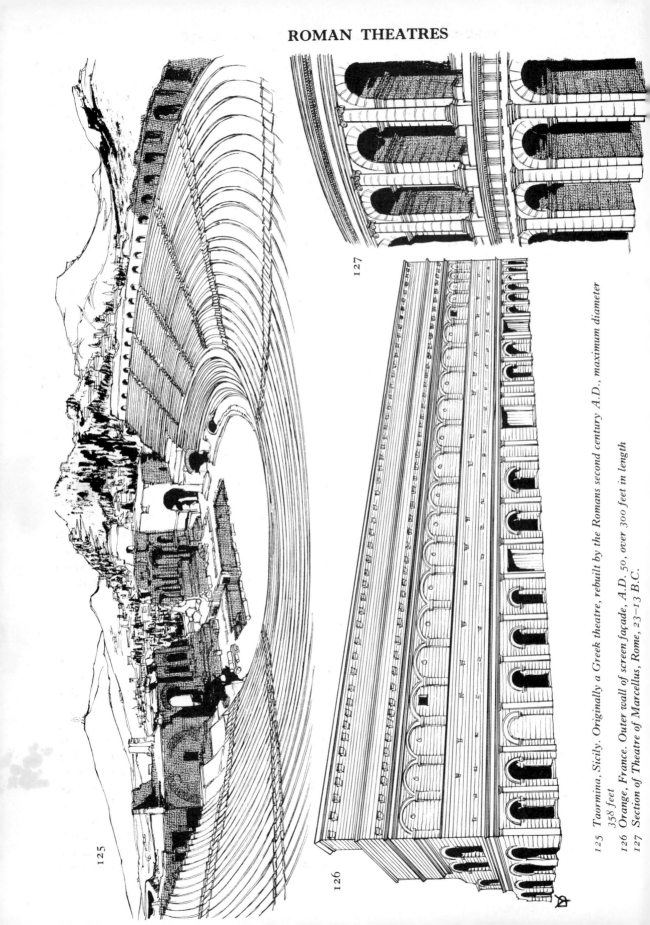

125 Taormina, Sicily. Originally a Greek theatre, rebuilt by the Romans second century A.D., maximum diameter 358 feet
126 Orange, France. Outer wall of screen façade, A.D. 50, over 300 feet in length
127 Section of Theatre of Marcellus, Rome, 23–13 B.C.

There are remains of many examples of thermae, particularly in Rome. Large establishments were built by most emperors, particularly Nero A.D. 60–71, Titus A.D. 80, Trajan A.D. 110, and Constantine A.D. 320. The most important remains are those of Caracalla A.D. 206–17 and Diocletian A.D. 284–304. These two famous examples in Rome illustrate the general layout of the extensive type of baths. There are a number of good reconstruction drawings of them and a clear idea of their appearance can be gained from the sixteenth century measured drawings by Renaissance architects like Palladio which were made when the remains were in a better condition than they are now.

The Baths of Caracalla, Rome A.D. 206–17

These thermae covered a very large area, greater than that of the Palace of Westminster, and stood upon an artificial platform some 20 feet high. Under the main buildings were vaulted cellars for storage and furnaces. Under the pavement of the baths was a lower floor upon which were built small piers of tiles about two feet high. These piers carried an intermediate concrete floor about one foot thick on which was a layer of broken and pounded tufa and ceramic. Upon this was laid a course of marble cement in which the mosaic pavement was bedded; alternatively marble slabs were laid. The furnaces were set lower still, below the hypocaust floor. The heated air passed under the mosaic floor and was carried by flues to the walls. In the caldarium flue pipes were laid all through the walls. The main building block of the Caracalla thermae is now in ruins but the plan and layout are still clearly to be seen. The area covered is 270,000 square feet of which the immense central hall occupied 79 feet by 183 feet. This is generally called the tepidarium but it is doubtful that it was in fact such a room for it would have been too immense to heat and no hypocausts have been discovered under it. The hall was covered by an intersecting barrel vault and was divided into three bays. It rose higher than the surrounding buildings and it was lit by clerestory windows below roof level. The vault was supported on eight massive stone piers fronted by granite columns 38 feet high. Next to the central hall was a smaller tepidarium and, beyond, the caldarium which had a domed roof. The frigidarium was presumed to be open to the sky and contained a large open-air swimming bath. On each side of the bath, separated from it by a colonnade, were halls for spectators. Although the exterior of this building was plain in brick and stucco, the interior was magnificent in colour and decoration with marble faced walls and floors and a wealth of sculpture and relief ornamentation much of which was brought from Greece. During Renaissance excavations many examples were taken from here to museums in Rome and other European cities.

The Baths of Diocletian, Rome. A.D. 284–304

These thermae were larger than those of Caracalla and accommodated 3200 bathers; they were very similar in design.

They are, however, particularly interesting to us as they are not entirely in ruins, because in A.D. 1563 Michelangelo converted the tepidarium into the nave of his Church, Santa Maria degli Angeli and retained the circular caldarium as an entrance vestibule with its domical roof now decorated with caissons and central roses. The nave of three bays has also retained the original vault though the marble facing has gone. However, a good impression can be gained of the original chamber as windows have been inserted under the vault above the Renaissance entablature and provide a well lighted interior. The main buildings here, as at Caracalla, were surrounded by gardens and gymnasia.

Baths at Pompeii

Three sites of public baths have been excavated here. They are smaller and less well equipped than the large Roman establishments but, being in a much better state of preservation, have provided invaluable material for study. The oldest layout at Pompeii is the *Stabian Baths*, built in the second century B.C. and remodelled later. The finest example is that adjacent to the forum, the *Forum Baths*. Here there is an open court with peristyle, the usual shops lining the site and the bathing rooms, ante-room and vestibule. The tepidarium is in a remarkable condition and still possesses a barrel vaulted ceiling with rich stucco decoration, stucco ornamented walls and, on piers surrounding the room, the figures of miniature Atlantes two feet high (PLATE 14). There was no hypocaust here; heating was by charcoal brazier. The frigidarium is small and circular in plan. The caldarium, also in good condition, had a hypocaust and wall flues; it is also barrel vaulted and stucco decorated (**105** and **150**).

Ostia

In the *Baths of Neptune* here there are some magnificent mosaic pavements in a fine state of preservation. There are two large examples, one in the entrance hall depicting Neptune driving four sea-horses surrounded by tritons, nereids, dolphins and other marine animals and, in the adjoining room, the mosaic shows Amphitrite with four tritons. There are remains of basins and columns in both tepidarium and caldarium. Next to the baths is the palaestra (gymnasium), which is a vast courtyard with surrounding colonnade and changing rooms. In the *Forum Baths,* on the other side of the town, the frigidarium is quite well preserved with remains of columns and capitals (**89**). Nearby is the public latrine with its 20 marble seats, washing facilities and holes in the entrance doorway floor for the two revolving doors (**156** and PLATE 23).

Theatres, Amphitheatres and Circuses

Theatres

The Roman theatre, when built on a new site, differed from the Greek pattern in that it was generally constructed above ground and not hollowed out from the hillside. Concrete vaulting supported the tiers of seats as in an amphitheatre and under the vaults were corridors lit by outer arcades. The orchestra was restricted to a semi-circle in view of the needs of Roman drama and, in front of this was a raised stage. The auditorium was also lined up on a semi-circular plan (**128**). In a number of instances the Romans took over a Greek theatre (for example at Taormina) and adapted it to their requirements. Thus the theatre was still built into the hillside, but the stage was constructed and the orchestral area curtailed.

128 Typical Roman theatre plan (simplified)

Theatre of Marcellus, Rome, *23–13 B.C.*

This is the only ancient theatre left in Rome; its masonry is now in a poor state. It is built in the Roman manner on a level site and the auditorium seats are supported on radiating walls and concrete vaulting. Only two tiers of the wall arcade remain showing the use of the Doric Order below and the Ionic above. They are built of travertine covered with stucco. The proportions and detail of these orders are some of the best work of its type in Rome and illustrate clearly the Roman constructional method using arch and order together with the former bearing the load and the latter as a decorative feature (**127**).

Orange, France, *A.D. 50*

This theatre, which is in good condition, is partly hollowed out from the hillside and partly constructed. The diameter between the enclosing walls is 340 feet. The important remaining feature here is the massive outer façade screen wall, 324 feet long and 116 feet high, constructed of large, squared blocks, about three feet long and one foot six inches wide. Remains of the entablature and Doric pilasters are distinguishable in the ground arcade (**126**).

Taormina, Sicily

This was a Greek theatre, hollowed out of the steep mountainside and looking out over one of the finest views in the world, with the sea far below on one side and, in the distance, Mount Etna. The Roman superstructure replanning has largely obscured the Greek design. In the Middle Ages much of the marble was taken for building and nineteenth century restoration has

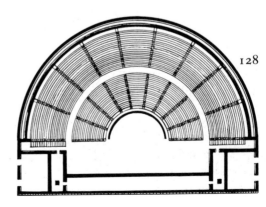

128

Plate 23 Public toilet facilities at Ostia, Port of Rome, second to fourth century A.D. Marble seating over running water supply

Plate 24 Latrines at the Roman fort at Housesteads on Hadrian's Wall, England

ROMAN AMPHITHEATRES

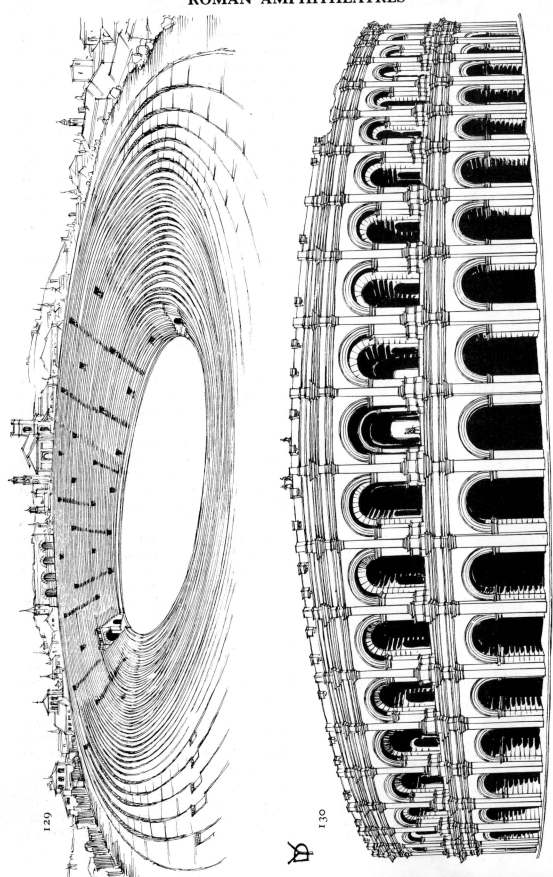

129 Amphitheatre at Verona, Italy, temp. Diocletian, c. A.D. 300, interior of arena viewed from back row, exterior measurement 498 ft × 404 ft
130 Amphitheatre at Nîmes, France, exterior arcade, exterior measurement 436 ft × 331 ft
131 Amphitheatre at Pula, Yugoslavia

129

130

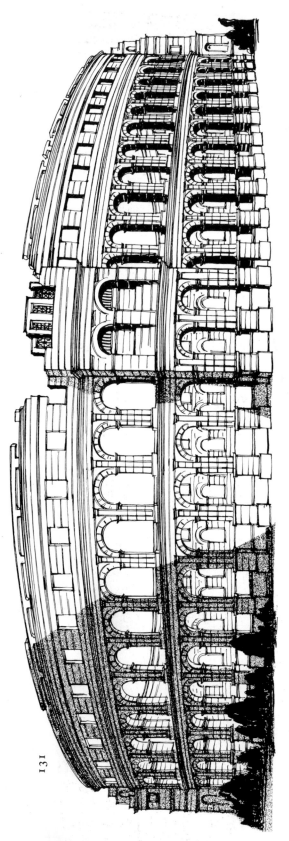

131

further confused the original layout. The Roman stage remains in ruined form and has curtailed the orchestra to a semi-circle, but the seating of the auditorium shows the Greek plan carved out of the hillside (**125**).

At *Pergamon* (Bergama) in Asia Minor is the beautifully situated Greek theatre. The scena still shows the three rows of square holes made to take the wood plank fittings when the moveable stage was in use. The Roman adaptation included the building of a large, permanent stage, 30 yards long, with accompanying terrace and porticoes 275 yards long. Among other interesting examples are those at *Mérida* in Spain (*c.* 18 B.C.) and *Verulamium* (S. Albans) in England (2nd century A.D.).

Amphitheatres

These were unknown to the Greeks and are peculiarly Roman constructions. Early examples were made of wood, but, due to fire risks, stone and concrete were used later. Most amphitheatres were very large and all important towns possessed their own which were used for displays of all kinds but particularly for gladiatorial combat and exhibitions. The plan is oval and rising tiers of seats are constructed round the elliptical area. The earliest known example is at Pompeii and the largest is the Colosseum. There are a number of fine amphitheatres extant in a partly ruined condition and several of them are still used for performances of opera or for bull fights. Among them are those at Verona, Capua and Pozzuoli in Italy, Nîmes and Arles in France, Pula in Yugoslavia and Pergamon in Turkey.

The Colosseum, Rome, A.D. 70–82
(also known as the Flavian Amphitheatre after the Flavian Emperors Vespasian, Titus and Domitian under whose auspices it was built).

Even in ruin the Colosseum is a magnificent edifice of great structural interest and aesthetic splendour. The interior is in a poor state but much of the four tiers of the exterior arcade walling is intact and illustrates clearly the Roman building method of using arch and order, with the entablatures continuing in unbroken horizontal bands round the whole amphitheatre and the columns lined up one above the other. In this instance on the ground storey is the Doric Order and above this, in order of ascent, Ionic, Corinthian and Corinthian. The fourth tier was originally in wood and was rebuilt in stone in the third century A.D. Between the three-quarter columns are arched openings, 80 on each of the first three storeys, and in each was placed a statue. The top storey has no openings and the order is in pilaster form. Between these pilasters are still visible the corbels upon which were supported the masts of the velarium which was drawn across the auditorium. This was a covering curtain with a central aperture which left the arena open to the sky. The façade is built of travertine blocks without mortar but held by metal cramps. It is 157 feet high and the amphitheatre from wall to wall is 620 by 513 feet, the largest in existence.

The construction is interesting and throws light on the Roman methods of dealing with the problem of erecting such a structure on a level site to accommodate some 45,000 to 50,000 people. The solid foundations are largely of volcanic materials, the supporting walls of brick tufa and travertine and the vaults of more porous volcanic substance to reduce weight. Decoration seating and the orders are in marble. The supporting construction consists of wedge-shaped piers which are set to radiate inwards. These support concrete vaults which slope downwards towards the arena. The access to seats is well arranged by means of staircases built between the walls and by passages between the seat ranges. The arena itself, some 287 by 180 feet, was encircled by a wall 15 feet high. The floor was carried on joists and under this was space for storage, scenery, gladiators and animals.

The tremendous solidity of the construction accounts for the substantial remains today. In fact the Colosseum has suffered less from the depredations of the barbarians and the weathering of time than from its use in the Middle Ages as a fortress and later as a quarry by Renaissance builders (**91** and **121**).

Amphitheatre at Verona A.D. 290

The arena here is in an exceptionally fine state of preservation, with nearly all the seats intact, and it is frequently used for modern performances. However, only four bays of the upper section of the exterior screen wall are *in situ*. The amphitheatre measures 498 by 404 feet from exterior wall to wall (**129**).

Amphitheatres in France

At *Nîmes* the exterior wall, measuring 436 by 331 feet across, is in only two storeys above which is an attic used for supporting the masts of the velarium. The Doric Order is used on both stages, as three-quarter piers on the ground storey and as three-quarter columns above. In each case the entablature is returned at each column. Both the exterior wall and the auditorium seating are in good condition and the amphitheatre is in use particularly for bull fights (**130**). At *Arles* nearby the screen wall is not in such good condition; the design is similar but the Corinthian Order is used instead of Doric (PLATE 26).

Yugoslavia

At *Pula* the exterior walling is in a fair state of complete preservation but the seating has disappeared; it was probably of wood. The masonry of the screen wall is rusticated and the orders are treated like those of the Colosseum, but in this case are less strongly defined. There are four projecting bays on the exterior with arcades in the ground storey and staircases in the upper storeys. The amphitheatre measures 450 by 361 feet (**131**).

Circuses

The Roman circus was used for chariot and horse races and was probably based, in plan, upon the Greek Stadion. There were many famous examples, but little is left of any of them except in such cities as *Rhodes*, where some twentieth century excavations and restoration have been carried out. The famous circuses were those built by different emperors in *Rome*, particularly those of Nero, Maxentius and Constantine. A very large example was the Circus Maximus, rebuilt by Julius Caesar and restored by later emperors. The circus built by Maxentius was called the Circus of Romulus and was 1620 feet long and 245 feet wide. The plan of this can still be determined.

Plate 25   Marble seats, theatre of Dionysos, Athens. Mainly fifth and fourth centuries B.C.

Plate 26   Amphitheatre, Nîmes, France, first century A.D. Ambulatory corridor on first floor

132   Ionic circular portico of the 'Maritime Theatre'
      (Ninfeo dell' Isola), Hadrian's Villa, near Tivoli
133   Temple of Hadrian, Ephesus, A.D. 130
134   Caryatid figure, Canopus, Hadrian's Villa

Palaces

Rome

There are only scanty remains of any of the great palaces despite the quantity and richness of the building over several centuries. The favourite position in Rome chosen by the emperors was the *Palatine Hill* although, by the time of Constantine, it was necessary to search further afield because of lack of space. Augustus laid out the first Imperial residence in this part of Rome, followed by Tiberius, Caligula and Domitian; Septimius Severus built here on a very large scale. Nero constructed his Imperial Villa—the famous 'golden house'—which he began soon after the great fire of the city in A.D. 64. This colossal layout covered an area larger than the present S. Peter's and the Vatican gardens and had an imperial entrance approach from the Forum. The palace was destroyed after Nero's death to make way for later Imperial building and the Colosseum was erected on the site of its lake. Despite excavations on the Palatine Hill which have continued since 1863 and which have uncovered a wide area, it is still difficult to ascertain clearly the design of these palaces. Remains are scanty and conjecture has to take the place of evidence. The palaces were very large, richly decorated and comprised a temple(s), basilica, public rooms, banqueting hall, a throne room and magnificent gardens with peristyle and fountains.

Tivoli

Of greater interest for its extensive remains is *Hadrian's Villa*, which the Emperor began to build near here, in A.D. 118, over several square miles of terraced hillside. Villa is a misnomer, for it included several thermae, stadia, halls, theatres, magnificent gardens, terraces and fountains as well as the imperial apartments. Hadrian was an outstanding architect himself, and here he gave vent to one of his interests.

Most of the marble and treasures have gone—destroyed, re-used or now in museums—but a clearer idea can be gained here than elsewhere of what such Roman palaces were like. Especially interesting is the layout known as 'Canopus'. Hadrian based this on the Temple of Serapis and the Canal of Canopus in the city of that name near Alexandria, where the cult of the god Serapis flourished. In his villa, the Serapeum is a vast semi-circular hall covered with a half-dome, originally worked in white mosaic. Much of the sculpture found on the site has now been placed *in situ* by the archaeologists: for example, the caryatid figures along the Canopus canal, which were copies from the famous ones on the south porch of the Erechtheion in Athens (**134** and PLATE 11).

An adequate description of the Villa Adriana would need a fair-sized guide-book. The most complete, and therefore, more interesting remains, include the Maritime Theatre and the Library, the Hall with the square Doric pillars and the Piazza D'Oro or Golden Square. Leading from the Library, the visitor enters a circular building, about 45 yards in diameter with an outer Ionic portico. Inside is a circular canal enclosing a small island on which was built a fine pavilion with domed halls and a central fountain. It is believed that this was Hadrian's retreat, where he went to be quiet and enjoy his drawing, writing and music-making. The island was originally joined to the circular portico by two small wooden bridges of a revolving, pulley type. The present stone bridge is a modern one. The names of 'Maritime Theatre' and 'Island Nymphaeum' derive from the entrance hall decoration with motifs of tritons, nereids and other marine life (**132**).

The Palace of Diocletian, Split, Yugoslavia

In about A.D. 300 the Emperor Diocletian built a palace here and to it he retired in about 305. As Hadrian's villa is much more than a villa, so Diocletian's palace is more like a town and is also designed as a fortress. The north, east and west walls are protected by 16 towers, the south by the sea. The palace site is rectangular and comprises a large part of the original Medieval town of Split. It is about 700 feet long on the east and west sides and about 580 feet on the north and south. In the centre of each side is an entrance gateway, flanked by octagonal towers, of which the principal one is the Porta Aurea (the Golden Gate) on the north side (**138**). The Porta Argentea on the seaward, south side is connected to the interior of the palace by an underground passage way. On the east and west sides are the Porta

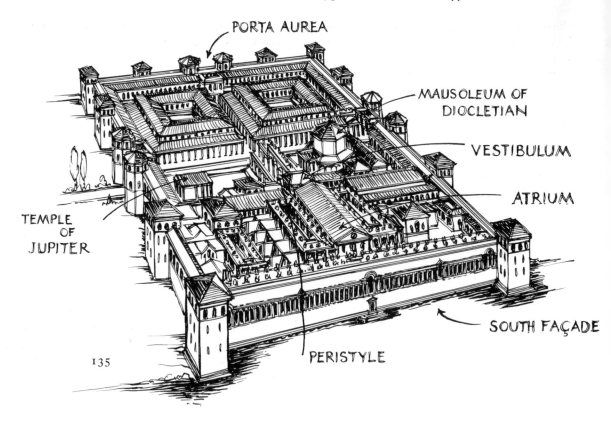

PORTA AUREA

MAUSOLEUM OF
DIOCLETIAN

VESTIBULUM

ATRIUM

TEMPLE
OF
JUPITER

SOUTH FAÇADE

135

PERISTYLE

135 Suggested reconstruction of the Palace of Diocletian, Split

Aenea and Ferrea (bronze and iron) respectively. These gateways gave entrance to avenues with covered arcades on each side which led to the centre of the enclosure.

The Palace, a reconstruction of which is shown in Fig. **135**, was built of limestone in a little over 10 years. It was beautiful and luxurious and designed both as status symbol and for ease of living for the emperor himself. In the time of Diocletian the principal apartment was a long gallery on the south side facing the sea on whose façade a magnificent colonnade stretched along the Adriatic. Within the palace walls were temples, baths, living accommodation, reception halls and gardens. In the centuries between the collapse of the Roman Empire and the present time Split has lived under many regimes and nationalities. It is astonishing, considering this turbulent history, that the remains of the palace are so extensive today. For the layout shows a Roman palace left almost complete with much of the walls, towers and gates standing. Inside the walls among Medieval and later houses, are considerable remains of Roman buildings and

careful excavation in recent times is still disclosing more of the semi-underground parts of the palace itself.

To the visitor who approaches the south side of the palace today from the harbour of Split the once magnificent *south wall and colonnade* are disappointing and a clearer idea of the original splendour of this elevation can be gained from Robert Adam's drawing made in 1764 before the shops were built in front of it at ground level. However, after entering through the underground tunnel in this façade a clear idea of Roman construction can be gained from the restored vaulted chambers which now lead up into the peristyle courtyard. There is a complex layout of these *basement halls* which were built to support the upper storey state apartments. The latter were almost completely destroyed, but the basement halls, still being excavated, survived almost intact (except for their decoration) due to their use over the centuries as the city refuse dump. The halls vary in size and shape— circular, octagonal, rectangular, apsidal—but all are vaulted in dome, barrel or groined forms constructed in brick, stone and concrete. The walls are thick and have arches with radiating voussoirs in brick (**140**). The *peristyle* is in a remarkable state of preservation and much as Robert Adam saw it, as can be seen by comparing his drawing of 1764 with Fig. **141** drawn in 1964. The Corinthian Order is used throughout this open central court which gave access from the southern gate below to the state apartments above (PLATE 21). It also served as an open ceremonial hall. Next to the peristyle still stands the *Emperor's Mausoleum*, preserved by its transformation into the Cathedral in the early Middle Ages. The Cathedral has not obscured the Mausoleum; on the exterior the octagonal form remains with the surrounding colonnade of Corinthian columns. In places are fragments of the coffered roof which originally connected the colonnade to the building which rests on an octagonal plinth once flanked by sphinxes (one of these is still extant) (**136** and **137**). A Medieval campanile has been added to one end of the Mausoleum and a Choir at the other. The *interior* still retains its original brick domed roof though its mosaic inlay has gone. The brick relieving arches are still visible above the entablature. The interior walls are alternately recessed with square and semicircular niches and there are eight columns of the Corinthian order supporting an entablature, with, above, eight further columns of the Composite order. A frieze, richly sculptured, encircles the building in the upper entablature; included in the decoration are sculptured medallions of Diocletian and his wife. While the Mausoleum is on the east of the peristyle, on the west were originally a number of temples of which the *Temple of Jupiter* is the only one to have survived. Apart from the loss of its columns it is in fine condition and has richly decorated doorway (**139**) and, inside, a barrel vaulted, coffered ceiling, its caissons finely enriched with flowers and heads. It was later made into a Christian baptistery. Of the *external walls* and *gates* of the palace, the west wall is missing and a number of towers. On the north side, however, dominated by Meštrović's colossal statue of Bishop Gregory, the whole length of the wall is intact. Its gate, the *Porta Aurea* (Golden Gate) is in good condition. It is interesting to notice here indications of the decadence of the late Roman style in the relieving

arches accentuated over a lintel and columns supported on corbels (**138**).

Domestic Architecture

There are very few remains of this type of building in Roman cities, particularly in Rome itself. Therefore great reliance in these studies is placed on the excavated sites of Pompeii, Herculaneum and Ostia where, due largely to natural causes, the site was abandoned, preserved, not rebuilt and excavated in more modern times. Of these, Pompeii especially was a provincial town, but the chief difference between it and Rome would be in the materials and embellishments used rather than in the basic design.

There were three chief types of Roman domestic building: the *domus* or private house, the villa (country house) and the *insula*, the multi-storeyed tenement. At Pompeii and Herculaneum there are examples of the *domus* and the villa while at Ostia can be seen considerable remains of *insulae*.

Pompeii

The story of the abrupt curtailment of life in Pompeii by the eruption of Vesuvius in A.D. 79 and the subsequent preservation of the city, not only its architecture but of the stuff of life itself— bread, utensils, eggs and bodies of humans, dogs and birds—through the protection of its coating of lava and ash is a well known one and has been fully and vividly recounted many times from the eye-witness story of Pliny himself to the present day. It is an exciting and fascinating story and one which the visitor to excavated Pompeii seems to re-live. From the architectural viewpoint the greatest importance of this site, now so excellently opened up and preserved, is that it has preserved for us a provincial Roman city at a certain point in time—A.D. 79—so that we can see for ourselves the buildings in which such citizens of the empire lived. No later buildings, no later civilisations with different ideas of development and design have pulled down, altered or erased the architecture remaining there.

Excavations have been continuing since the eighteenth century, and in the early years much was lost in plundering and in destruction by lack of knowledge of the work. In more modern times

LINE OF ATTACHMENT
OF ORIGINAL
COLONNADE
ROOF

137

138

136

139

141

140

136 *Mausoleum of Diocletian with surrounding colonnade*
    (now Cathedral)
137 *Corinthian capital from peristyle*
138 *The Porta Aurea*

139 *Doorway detail, Temple of Jupiter (now Baptistery)*
140 *Vestibulum. Underground approach to Peristyle*
    —brick and stone barrel vaults
141 *The Peristyle of the Palace*

POMPEII A.D. 79

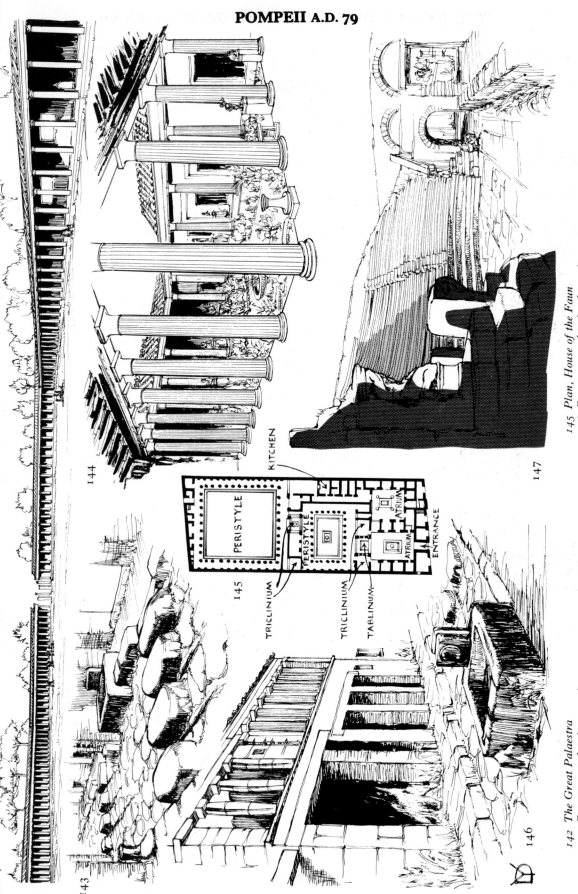

143

144

145

146 PERISTYLE

147

KITCHEN

PERISTYLE

TRICLINIUM

TRICLINIUM

TABLINUM

ATRIUM

ATRIUM

ENTRANCE

142 The Great Palaestra
143 Street scene showing stepping stones
144 Peristyle, House of the Vettii

145 Plan, House of the Faun
146 Street scenes showing fountains
147 The small theatre or odeon

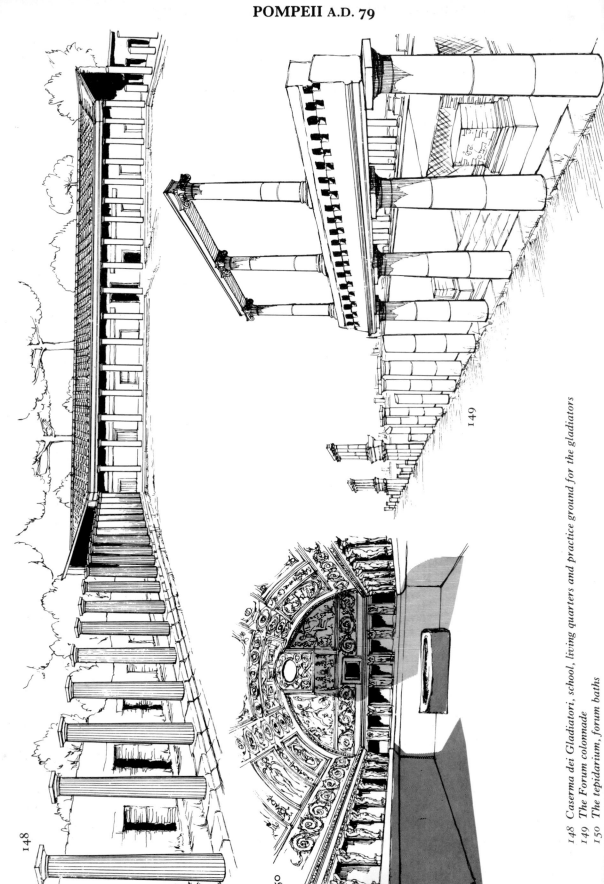

148

149

150

148 *Caserma dei Gladiatori, school, living quarters and practice ground for the gladiators*
149 *The Forum colonnade*
150 *The tepidarium, forum baths*

great care has been taken and it is a feature of Pompeii that where possible, having regard to the safety of the work, sculpture, mosaics and frescoes have been left *in situ*, giving a clear picture of the interiors of houses and baths. The domestic gardens have also been recreated in their original plan and types of plants; many of the fountains are in working order.

The *city*, which had about 20,000 inhabitants, is irregular to plan and enclosed by stone city walls of double thickness with earth and stones between. There are towers at intervals for reinforcement and there are eight fortified city gates which were originally richly decorated with sculptural work. The *main roads* within the city gates are paved with dark local stone and have pavements and kerbstones. Large stone blocks are set as stepping stones for pedestrians to cross without becoming muddied. There are also street fountains at intervals (**143** and **146**).

Considerable remains of houses and public buildings exist and the layout is clearly defined. The *forum*, which is the most complete example in Italy, conforms closely to Vitruvius' account of ideal planning for a forum and its position in a city. It is a rectangle 520 by 125 feet, surrounded by a colonnade on three sides; this is in two storeys, the lower one Doric, the upper Ionic. At one end is the Temple of Jupiter built on a high podium; the Corinthian Order is used and the building was flanked by two triumphal arches. Opposite this, at the other side of the forum, was the Curia. Nearby are the remains of the *Basilica* which was the most impressive building here. It had a large nave with massive columns separating it from the aisles (**92** and **93**). Adjoining the forum is the Temple of Apollo which is the best preserved temple at Pompeii; it had a portico of 48 columns and there is a fine statue of the god in the courtyard.

There are two theatres at Pompeii and an amphitheatre. The *large theatre* was hollowed out from the hillside in the Greek manner and has a magnificent situation with mountain background. It was used for plays and mimes and seated about 5000 people. The *small theatre* or odeon was covered and adjoins the larger one. This is in a fine state of preservation and still retains two male figures carved in the tufa forming the head of the side parapets of the auditorium (**147** and PLATE 19). The theatre was built in

about 80 B.C. and accommodated 1200. It was used chiefly for performances of reading and music. The *amphitheatre*, constructed in 70 B.C. is a very early example and the first one to be built in stone. It is elliptical and very large—445 by 341 feet—and was used, as was the custom, for gladiatorial combat, dancing and animal baiting. The training grounds and living quarters of the *gladiators* (Caserma dei Gladiatori) are extensive at Pompeii and adjoin the large theatre (**148**).

Houses

To facilitate the study of Roman houses the following list of common terms is given.

Atrium A large hall, lit by an opening in the centre of the roof called a *compluvium*. Rainwater ran from the eaves, through the gutters and spouted into a tank called the *impluvium*. Usually at one end of the tank was a sculptured figure from some part of which the water poured into the impluvium.

Bibliotheca Library.

Cubicula Sleeping apartments.

Culina Kitchen.

Exedrae Small rooms for reading and conversation.

Peristyle A large square or rectangular colonnaded space, open to the sky, and generally made into a garden with fountains and sculpture.

Pinacotheca Picture gallery.

Tablinum Large room generally richly decorated and sculptured.

Triclinium Dining room. Had couches on three sides; the fourth was for serving. The table was placed centrally.

It is in the field of domestic architecture that Pompeii is unique; the houses are in a remarkable state of preservation and, apart from Herculaneum and Ostia, there is so little of such building extant. The Pompeian house does, of course, only depict the Roman home of up to the first century A.D. and in later years, as can be seen at Ostia, the plan was developed. The houses at Pompeii vary greatly in size and elaboration, from two or three rooms to large buildings with many rooms arranged round courtyards. There are, however, a number of common features. The houses are entered from a narrow street façade

151 House of Diana (restoration)
152 Capital, Baths of Neptune
153 House of Diana, as it is today
154 Theatre, first-third century A.D.

155 Thermopolium (bar)
156 Public toilet facilities in the Forum Baths, facilities also for washing, revolving doors at entrance, second-fourth century A.D.

often fronted by shops. Within they are generally planned on a narrow rectangular site, extending a long way back from the road. The rooms are all grouped around one or more peristyles. In a number of the houses the staircase has been preserved and much of the upper floors; only the roof is missing. Among the many examples the *House of the Faun* is often considered to have a typical layout. It is a large house and has two entrances, each leading into an atrium. From the atria one passes into the first peristyle which has an Ionic colonnade and a central fountain. A corridor from an exedra leads into the second, larger peristyle which had a gallery over the colonnade. The living rooms are arranged round the atria. The whole layout is well designed, spacious and suitable for the climate. The rooms were richly decorated with wall paintings, mosaics and sculptural work (**145**).

Among other outstanding houses at Pompeii are the *House of Menander*, the *House of Pansa* and the *House of the Vettii*. In the last of these particularly, the peristyle has now been restored, as has the garden, and one gains a vivid impression of the original appearance (**144**). There are also a number of *villas* (country houses) at Pompeii and here the plan is quite different. While the town house was completely enclosed in four walls on a rectangular plan to provide privacy from the streets, the villa was built in a less formal manner on a large ground plan and had terraced gardens overlooking the Bay of Naples. The *Villa of the Mysteries* with its two symmetrical, galleried wings is typical of these beautiful houses.

Herculaneum, the twin city to Pompeii, suffered a similar fate but has proved more difficult to excavate. It was smaller, buried much deeper and the later town of Resina is built partly on top. There are some beautiful houses here, particularly those villas along the Bay of Naples where wealthy citizens (from other towns) wintered in a warm climate. These houses are laid out in terraces on the hillside with porticoes and colonnaded peristyles. There are also several storeyed tenements of the style excavated at Ostia and as were built in Rome.

Art in the form of sculpture, mosaics and painting has survived extremely well at Pompeii and Herculaneum; the lava has protected the work from the invasions, wars and plundering suffered by the rest of the Roman Empire after A.D. 476. Much of this work has been removed to museums for safe keeping, particularly to Naples. There are, however, a number of frescoes and mosaics *in situ* and they illustrate the Pompeian's love of rich colour and their knowledge of their craft. Mosaic, marble slabs, stucco and painted decoration covered a large area of the walls, ceiling and floor of each house. The work has vigour and good taste. It is strongly influenced by Greek and Etruscan artists and happily shows none of the degeneracy evident in some later Roman work (PLATES 14 and **19**).

Ostia

The story of Ostia is less generally known than that of Pompeii and Herculaneum. Yet, in many ways, events have created a similar situation: a town abandoned by humanity and then preserved by natural forces until excavation in modern times. The basic differences between them in respect of their value to architectural study is that Ostia was occupied and developed over a much longer period, from the fourth century B.C. to the third century A.D., and that it was not a provincial city but the port of Rome and, as such, became more important, as is evidenced by its buildings. The chief development period at Ostia was under the Empire, particularly under the Emperors Augustus, Tiberius, Claudius and Nero. The task of making Ostia into a large and suitable port to serve Rome with a tremendous quantity of goods, particularly salt and grain, continued over many years, and the building of harbours and dredging of the river were not completed until about A.D. 54. A fine city was then built, having a population of some 50,000 people, with well laid out streets, drainage system and many temples, public buildings, shops and houses. It was Constantine who transferred the municipal rights of the port of Rome to Porto and from this time onwards Ostia declined. By the fourth century buildings were neglected and the marble facings were being taken for building elsewhere. In the early sixth century the place was largely deserted and became a malaria infested area. In 1557 the Tiber changed its course and Ostia Antica (as it is termed to differentiate it from the modern Lido town) is now a few kilometres inland and not on the riverside any more.

Excavations are not yet complete at Ostia, but the main part of the town (though not the harbour) has been uncovered with its principal streets and buildings. The main street, the *Decumanus Maximus* is bordered by tombs until it reaches the city gate. Inside the gates it is flanked by colonnades and the principal buildings lie adjacent to it. This street is about a mile in length and runs from one end of the town to the other; it is ten yards wide. Sited by it are the *Baths of Neptune* (already described, see Baths, p. 52), the *Palaestra*, the theatre (**152, 154** and PLATE 18), and the *Piazzale delle Corporazioni*. This square is very large and was originally faced with 70 offices carrying on trade with the whole ancient world. The mosaic floors of each office depict the trade of the occupier (PLATE 20). In the centre of the square are the remains of the Temple of Ceres

It is in *domestic architecture* that Ostia provides the most interesting revelations for here are astonishingly well preserved remains of *insulae*, the *tenement blocks* which must have been constructed in quantity in Rome itself and, since Ostia is so near and as it had such close association with the capital, probably of a very similar character. It had long been thought that many seventeenth and eighteenth century blocks in Rome were of a type of construction essentially Medieval or Renaissance, but Ostia shows that the basic plan of these is Roman. Such blocks at Ostia were built in the Imperial period and housed a number of people. They were constructed up to a height of 50 feet in three or four storeys (height of buildings was limited by Roman law). Among examples of such apartment houses is the *Casa di Diana* in the street of the same name and that in the *Via dei Balconi*. Here is the typical layout of such blocks, which is quite different from the Pompeian house. At Ostia the block is much taller, generally four storeys high and the walls are brick faced. The entrances are marked by pilasters or engaged columns supported on a triangular gable. The decoration is in simple string courses and in painting of the doors and windows. Polychrome decoration is used also in the form of coloured brick and bands of pumice and tufa. The rooms are lit by windows on the exterior and in the courtyard walls and the rooms themselves are laid out much as in a modern flat. Some blocks

have covered arcades and shops on the ground floor and apartments above. Above the shops are projecting balconies which are supported either on wood or travertine corbels or are continuous along the whole façade. The interior courtyard is not like an atrium or peristyle. The windows, doors and staircases of the different storeys open on to it as in modern design. The staircases are of travertine with wooden treads. They descend into the courtyard or into the street. In the *Casa di Diana*, two storeys have been preserved; the street façade with shops on the ground floor, the second floor windows and above this the third floor balcony which projects along the length of the block. The interior courtyard has a fountain and there are fragments of terracotta and fresco paintings (**151, 153** and **155**). Nearby, in the *Casa dei Dipinti*, in the street of the same name some mosaic floors are still preserved and a hall painted with mythological scenes. The *domus* (private house) also existed at Ostia and examples resemble Pompeian houses. They have a narrow frontage to the street and are planned around an atrium and peristyle. Many have shops on the lower floor.

Greece and Turkey

There are extensive remains of Roman building in these countries, mainly where the Roman civilisation extended and altered earlier towns established under Greek culture. It is not always easy for the visitor to distinguish the Greek work from Roman in these instances, but in general much more Roman building survives than the earlier Greek.

In the second century B.C. the Romans had gained control of the Sacred island of *Delos* in the Cyclades and later established it as a commercial trading post in the Mediterranean. A forum, quays, harbours, villas, baths and theatres were constructed also a system of water conservation and control. Although the centre declined by the second century A.D., due largely to pirate raiding, the Roman remains are considerable.

In Asia Minor are a number of Greek towns which became Romanised and where excavation has revealed sites and building. *Ephesus* is one of the finest examples of these. There is a theatre, baths, the impressive library and an odeon mainly erected in the second century A.D. Like

Pompeii a number of streets have been uncovered, some marble paved and with remains on each side of shops, houses and public buildings. Two of these are the Via Arcadiana linking the theatre and the harbour and the Street of Kuretes which ascends the hill. The Temple of Hadrian is one of the buildings lining this thoroughfare (**133**).

Triumphal Arches and Columns of Victory

The arch is a typical form of Roman building and, in the design of monumental arches or town gateways, has survived better than any other feature of Roman architecture. The *triumphal arch* or, as it was earlier called the monumental arch, is the most typical of all the forms. Such arches were erected to commemorate important military or domestic happenings, or in memory and respect of generals and emperors. They were generally built astride a road and had one or three archways. The latter type provided a wide central opening for vehicular traffic and two smaller side ones for pedestrians. An order was used on the arch, usually with four columns or pilasters on each wide elevation; the common choice was Corinthian or Composite. The plinths below the columns, the arch spandrels, friezes and entablatures were enriched with carved ornament and sculpture. Above the cornice was an attic for the appropriate dedicatory inscription, while a large sculptural group surmounted the whole arch, usually in the form of a triumphal car with four or six horses flanked at the corners by statues. Several such arches were in the Forum Romanum and two remain, those of Titus and of Septimius Severus, while nearby, outside the Colosseum, is the Arch of Constantine. These are the most famous examples, in Rome but there are other excellent arches in Italy and other provinces at Ancona, Benevento, Rimini, Susa, Aosta and Orange.

The Arch of Titus, Rome (A.D. 81) is generally regarded as the finest of the extant triumphal arches, particularly of the single arched design. It is built across the Via Sacra at its summit, looking down on the Forum Romanum. It commemorates the capture of Jerusalem in A.D. 70 and in the two panels inside the central opening are represented the Emperor in his triumphal car and the spoils taken from the Temple (PLATE 17). The general design is a simple one and the standard of the sculpture and decoration is high. The Composite Order is used, the first known example of this (**97**). Since there is only one opening the base has a simple podium on each side instead of a series of pedestals. This gives strength to the design, which is also enhanced by the lofty attic, above which was originally a sculptured quadriga. The keystones are richly carved and the arch soffit is deeply coffered and enriched. The sides of the arch were destroyed in the Middle Ages when it was incorporated in the fortifications. Valadier restored them in 1821 in travertine which is distinguishable from the original marble workmanship (**157**). Also in the Forum Romanum is the *Arch of Septimius Severus* (A.D. 204); the best example of the three arched type triumphal arch. It was erected in honour of the Emperor and his two sons Caracalla and Geta for their victories in Mesapotamia. These events are depicted in four relief pictures above the side openings of the arch but are in a poor state of preservation. The arch spandrels are decorated by figures of winged victory and personifications of rivers. Originally the arch was surmounted by a six-horse chariot. The Composite Order is used; the columns stand on sculptured pedestals. The attic is large to accommodate the extensive inscription. Apart from the weathering of the sculpture, the arch has been well preserved due to the protection afforded in the Middle Ages from an adjacent church and fortifications (**159**).

The *Arch of Constantine* in *Rome* (A.D. 312) is a much later construction than the other two and is consequently larger and more richly decorated. The sculptural decoration, which is contemporary with the building of the arch, is cruder and poorer but much of the ornamentation was taken from earlier monuments in the period of Marcus Aurelius and Trajan. These Trajan and Antonine reliefs are of high standard. The arch has three openings divided by columns of the Corinthian Order based on sculptured pedestals; the entablature is returned over each column. The arch was built in honour of Constantine's victory over Maxentius (**158**).

In Italy, outside Rome, the *Arch of Trajan* in *Benevento* (A.D. 114) is a magnificent example which acts as a foundation for rich sculptural decoration which provides a pictorial history of Trajan's life and policy. It is a well preserved

157

158

159

160

161

162

157 Arch of Titus, Rome, Composite, A.D. 81
158 Arch of Constantine, Corinthian, A.D. 312
159 Arch of Septimius Severus, Forum Romanum, Rome, Composite, A.D. 204
160 Arch of Tiberius, Orange, France, Corinthian, c. 30 B.C.
161 Porta Nigra, Trier, Germany, Town Gateway, Tuscan, early fourth century
162 Arch of Augustus, Rimini, Italy, Corinthian, 27 B.C.

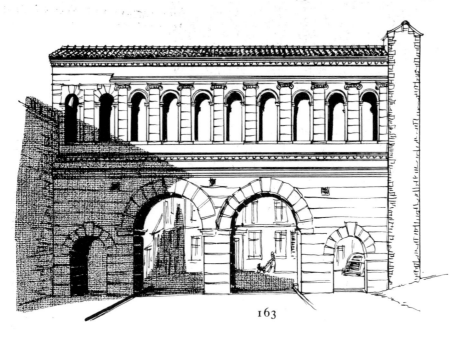

163 *Porte S. André, Autun, France*

163

arch using the Composite Order. The *Arch of Trajan* in *Ancona* (A.D. 113) was set up at the harbour entrance astride a causeway. It is approached by a flight of steps and has a high podium. The sculptural group for which it was originally intended as a pedestal has now gone and the proportion of the arch appears too tall and narrow. The *Arch of Augustus* in *Rimini* (27 B.C.) is a very early and simple structure. It is a single arch with large voussoirs. The decoration is restrained and, apart from the Corinthian Order, is seen in the medallions in the spandrels. The arch was built to commemorate Augustus' restoration of the chief highways of Italy (**162**).

Outside Italy, one of the finest examples is the *Arch of Tiberius* at *Orange* in *France* (c. 30–20 B.C.). It straddles the main road into Orange, but a large roundabout has been constructed for the arch to stand serenely in a wide circular grass plot in the centre of the pounding traffic. This is a very early example of a three-arched design, in the Corinthian Order. The sides and arch panels are sculptured and there is a rich coffered vault under the central opening (**109** and **160**). The *Arch of Galerius* in *Thessaloniki* in Greece is also interesting (PLATE 16).

Town Gateways

There are a number of arches extant which were built as entrances to towns or bridges, or formed part of the fortified town walling. Most of these in Italy are in a poor condition as in Rome, Ascoli, Pompeii, Ostia, etc. but the provinces have fared better. In *France* there is the *Porte de Mars* at *Reims* and two gateways at *Autun*. Here the *Porte S. André* has four archways, two larger ones for traffic and two smaller for pedestrians. It is surmounted by an arcaded gallery with Ionic pilasters. It is still in use as the town gateway as is the other example on the other side of the town which uses the Corinthian Order (**163**). At *Split* in *Yugoslavia* the *Porta Aurea* in the Palace of Diocletian has already been referred to (**138**), and in *Spain* at *Alcántara*, the Roman bridge still possesses its portal over the central pier (**167**). Probably the most interesting of these provincial archways is the *Porta Nigra* at *Trier* in *Germany* built in A.D. 275. It was part of the city walls but now, like the arch at Orange, stands in a protected island from the surrounding traffic. It consists of an outer and inner gateway with two storeys of arcading having engaged columns between in the Tuscan-Doric Order. It is flanked by two towers four storeys high (one of which has been damaged and has only three storeys left). Much of the interior remains and can be visited and explored. This archway is different from other examples and possesses a Romanesque quality rather than a Roman (**161**).

ROMAN BRIDGES

164 Bridge at Mérida, Spain, over River Guadiana. 60 arches over half a mile. The longest surviving example
165 Bridge and the two cathedrals at Salamanca, Spain. River Tormes
166 Ponte Fabrizio, Rome, 69–21 B.C. Spans half of River Tiber to the Isola Tiberina in centre of river

164

165

166

Columns of Victory

Like the triumphal arches these were erected in honour of victorious generals. The two most famous examples are in *Rome*: the Trajan Column and the Antonine Column. The *Trajan Column* was built by the Greek architect *Apollodorus* of Damascus, like the rest of the Trajan Forum, and was set next to the basilica there in A.D. 114. It is a remarkable column surmounted by a Doric capital which is in one block of marble 14 feet square and nearly five feet high (**101**). The column itself is decorated by a long relief frieze wound round from top to bottom and representing episodes from the Emperor's Dacian campaigns. It is over 800 feet long and contains some 2500 human figures. The standard of work is high as can be seen from a small section shown in PLATE 15. The *Antonine Column to Marcus Aurelius* erected in *c*. 180 is very similar in design and commemorates the Emperor's victory on the Danube. The Doric Order is also used and the column is the same height as the Trajan one, that is 115 feet. The sculptural work is vastly inferior and is so high in relief as to be almost in the round (**88**).

Bridges and Aqueducts

Roman bridges were well and simply designed and solidly constructed. Most surviving examples are in well laid, massive stonework, while more rarely concrete with brick facings is used. The roadway is level throughout. Examples can be found in different parts of the empire. In *Rome* there were originally 11 bridges over the Tiber; nearly all of these have been modernised or replaced. The oldest surviving example is the *Pons Fabricius* (Ponte Fabrizio) built 62–21 B.C. and spanning half of the river from the main bank to the Isola Tiberina, near the Theatre of Marcellus. There are two semi-circular arches and, between, an opening over the central pier for flood water (**166**). Also in *Italy* is the beautiful single-arched bridge at *Ascoli Piceno* and, at *Rimini*, the *Bridge of Augustus* (Tiberius) still bears the heavy traffic of the Via Flaminia over the River Marecchia. The latter was built in A.D. 14 and is the best preserved example in Italy. It has five arches with pedimented niches between and with a parapet above. In Spain are three famous bridges; one is at *Alcántara*, built in A.D. 105 by Hadrian over the River Tagus. This is a most impressive structure. In wild, rocky countryside, it is 650 feet long, with a level roadway throughout, over six arches in granite blocks superbly laid without mortar. A dam is now being constructed just upstream from the bridge. It intrudes on the isolation of the scene and reduces the Tagus flow but presents an

167 Bridge over the River Tagus at Alcántara, Spain, A.D. 105–6

168 *Pont du Gard, Nîmes, France. Built by Agrippa, 18–19 B.C.*
169 *Puente de las Ferraras (also called Puente del Diavolo) Tarragona, Spain. Temp. Trajan. Double arcade of 11 and 25 arches*

170 Roman Aqueduct at Segovia, Spain. Temp. *Augustus*

interesting contrast in engineering achievement, ancient and modern (**167**). Another example exists at *Salamanca* (**165**) and there is a very long, many-arched bridge at *Mérida* (**164**).

The Roman system of supplying water to cities by means of *aqueducts* above ground presented an engineering problem. Such monumental works that are extant in all parts of the empire are without decoration of any kind, but consist simply of arch after arch for miles across the landscape, presenting an impressive and significant spectacle of considerable aesthetic quality, as important in the study of Roman architecture as, for example, the Colosseum. The Romans attached great importance to an adequate supply of good water for their fountains, baths and domestic use. In Rome alone, it has

been estimated that over 340 million gallons a day were needed from the 11 great aqueducts which poured into the city. These were built across the Campagna and surrounding areas, many miles in length, simply yet grandly constructed. With slave labour they were cheaper to build than it was to provide the necessary lead or bronze piping for alternative means. The supporting arches were often in tiers, sometimes of great height, while the water ran in a cement-lined channel in the top. According to Vitruvius, a fall of six inches over every 100 feet was considered desirable and often long detours had to be made to avoid a too sudden descent.

Of the extant examples the best known in *Italy* is the *Acqua Claudia* (meaning the eighth) built A.D. 36–50 from Subiaco across the Campagna to Rome. It is 44 miles long and for nearly nine miles of this distance is borne on arches up to 100 feet high. A number of lengths remain in the Campagna.

The finest aqueduct is the *Pont du Gard* near *Nîmes* in *France*. This is a comparatively short section, in a beautiful setting, of an original aqueduct 25 miles long. It was constructed by Agrippa in 18–19 B.C. and consists of two tiers of arches each about 65 feet high and an upper tier of smaller arches 28 feet high. The water channel is four feet wide inside and is covered by slabs of stone over cemented sides. This section is *c.*

900 feet long and crosses the valley 180 feet above the River Gard. The main road still uses the bridge on the first tier and one can walk along the full length of the water channel (**168**). There are some fine aqueducts in *Spain* notably at *Segovia, Tarragona* and *Seville*. Those at Segovia and Tarragona cross deep valleys and are of great height in two tiers of arches, the lower tier being much taller than the upper. At *Segovia* the aqueduct bridge is 2700 feet long and 102 feet high formed with 118 arches constructed in granite blocks without mortar. The aqueduct is still in use (**169** and **170**).

3
Early Christian and Byzantine: 325–1453

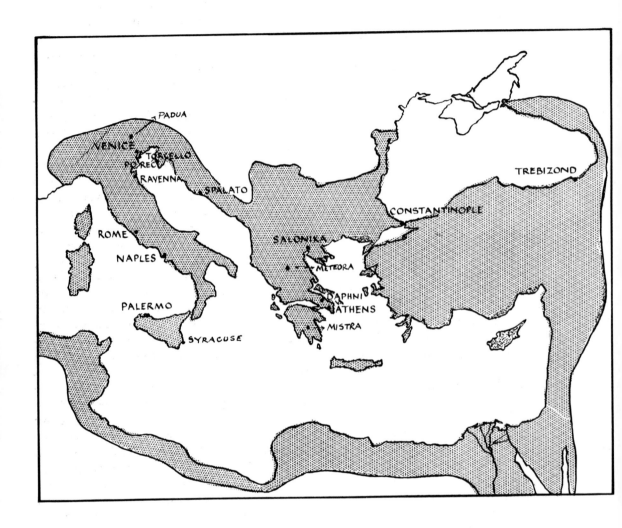

The interest and achievement of Byzantine architecture is in the wide spread of its influence in Europe and in its vital importance as a link, both structurally and aesthetically, between the work of Ancient Rome and the emergence of Romanesque. A glance at the sketch map above will show the general limits of the Byzantine Empire (which fluctuated greatly during this long period), but the influence of the style was exerted over a much greater area: north to Russia, north-west to southern France, east to Armenia and Georgia.

The *characteristics* of Byzantine design remained almost constant during this extended time but there were two chief phases of development, based upon the periods of expansion and wealth of the Empire. These were the fifth and sixth centuries, when Byzantine designs were forming themselves from early Christian patterns, and the tenth to thirteenth centuries when more elaborate buildings were erected in a new wave of expansion. To the earlier age belong the churches at Ravenna and those on the Istrian Peninsula and also Santa Sophia at Istanbul; to the later, many of the Greek, Serbian and Russian churches as well as the Cathedral of S. Mark in Venice. In this time, in the eleventh century, the Byzantine Empire flourished exceedingly and extended from the Euphrates to the Danube.

Extant remains of Byzantine architecture are largely in the form of churches and cathedrals and herein lies one of the chief differences between it and the preceding Roman epoch, which had produced much secular work as well as temples. The Byzantine Empire, with its capital at Byzantium (Istanbul), was strongly influenced by a number of contrasting elements: Christianity, which was the official religion; the Oriental factor from further east and the Hellenic force provided by a largely Greek population in the capital and surrounding area who, due to their heredity and training, provided the best craftsmen in building and decoration. The new culture of Byzantium, taking over from the dying Roman Empire, needed few secular buildings (except in the capital itself) for, although much had been destroyed, the population was greatly depleted. But the religion of the new Empire was Christianity and large numbers of churches were built, great and small, all over its domains, to the glory of God. Many of these were temples converted into Christian churches.

The structural link between Roman architecture and Romanesque was the Byzantine development of the *dome*. The Greeks had used the post and lintel principle—trabeated architecture; the Romans used the arch and vault together with the post and lintel and combined the trabeated and arcuated forms of construction. But they never fully developed the potentialities of the arch and rarely used the dome. When they did employ this form it was, as at the *Pantheon*, a dome set upon circular walls which did not present great constructional problems (**127, 128** and **129**). In Byzantine architecture was evolved the principle of the dome set over a square, first upon squinches which, built across the corners, provided an octagonal base for the dome, and later on pendentives. It is the pendentive which represents the great Byzantine contribution to structural form and enabled the large domed structures of Europe, from Russia to southern France, to be built. The construction of the pendentive is described on page 86 and illustrated

in Fig. **175**. It solved efficiently and finally the problem of how to construct a circular form upon a square one.

Early Christian Architecture

Until the early fourth century *Christianity* had been practised in secret in underground cellars and rooms. In A.D. 313 the *Emperor Constantine* issued the Edict of Milan which gave to Christians the right to practise their religion openly on an equal basis with other religions. In A.D. 325 the Emperor himself professed Christianity, which then became the official religion of the Roman Empire. It was from this time onward that Christian churches were built for the purpose of worship and a form of *Christian architecture* was begun. Until the fall of Rome in A.D. 476 such new churches were designed in Roman classical style and modelled upon the plan and construction of the *basilica*, the Roman hall of justice and administration. Such churches were, therefore, like the basilica, rectangular in plan, twice as long as wide and had two or four rows of columns set along the long axis, providing three or five aisles. At one end, generally the east, was an apse. The columns and capitals of the nave colonnade were frequently taken from ruined Roman buildings and are therefore different from one another and the capital does not fit its column or base. This colonnade carried a classical entablature and above was a plain wall (where the Medieval triforium normally is to be found) and above this a row of small clerestory windows. The ceiling was flat and of wood, simple but decoratively finished. The *basilican church* was generally built over the burial place of the saint to whom it was dedicated. The burial place was surrounded by the crypt and above it, in the church, was the high altar.

The term 'basilican' applied to churches and cathedrals is often loosely used and given to buildings of different plan and construction. A basilican church, like these early Christian ones, can be defined as one having the following features:

1. a rectangular not cruciform plan
2. therefore, no transepts
3. division into nave and aisles by columns not piers
4. an apse at one end of the nave called a *bema* (presbytery)

5. walls which are not reinforced and cannot bear a stone vault.

Early development of this basilican plan included the addition of a western *narthex* and a separate *baptistery*. In front of the church at the west end was built a portico or narthex which generally extended across the whole width of the façade. In front of this was usually the *atrium* or forecourt. The purpose of the narthex was to accommodate those, such as penitents, who were not permitted to enter the church, and to enable them to hear the service. Later designs further adapted the basilican plan with apses at both east and west ends and sometimes added short transepts. The baptistery was, in early Christian times, used only for the sacrament of baptism. At first only one or two were built in each city; they were large and generally on circular plan. By the fifth and sixth centuries they were set adjacent to larger churches, usually in the atrium facing the narthex.

Numerous *churches* were constructed in the fourth to sixth centuries after the establishment of Christianity as the official religion of Rome. Many of them were in Rome itself and many more in Italy and surrounding lands. Later, in the eastern part of the empire, the basilican plan gave place to Byzantine, Greek cross variations in layout, but in the west—Italy, France, England and Germany—basilicas continued to be built, even till today. Such churches were plain on the exterior but richly decorated inside. They were built mainly of brick but had columns, capitals, entablatures and wall coverings of marble and stone taken from the numerous ruined Roman secular buildings; most floors were of Roman mosaic. Such interior schemes were haphazard in design and sometimes incongruous but pleasantly and tastefully decorated.

Of the early basilicas, built in the second–fourth centuries A.D. none exists entirely unaltered, but sufficient survives or has been carefully rebuilt to the original pattern to give a clear idea of what such churches were like. *Rome* is the centre for most of these. The greatest examples have been lost completely: *Old S. Peter's*, built in 330 by Constantine, was replaced by the great basilica now standing on the same site, *S. John in Lateran* has been considerably altered.

Of the other great churches, *S. Maria Maggiore* has been extensively altered outside but its interior, built 432–40, still retains much of the original features including the 21-bay Ionic marble colonnade with its gilded arabesque frieze. Above are Corinthian pilasters and a gold and white coffered ceiling, erected in the sixteenth century. The floor is of white and grey marble patterned with black circles and diamonds. The altar is at the west end* where the apse is decorated with rich gilt and coloured mosaics which cover the whole surface area and, in the conch, is depicted Christ and the Virgin Mary. In front is the great triumphal arch, also mosaic faced, and the Baroque baldacchino.

S. Paul-outside-the-Walls (S. Paolo fuori le Mura), built in 380, is so called, as is S. Lorenzo, because both great basilicas were built outside the city walls of ancient Rome. It was the largest of the Roman basilicas until its destruction in 1823. It was then rebuilt to the original design and today gives a clear picture of the layout and impressiveness of such churches. The vast exterior is fronted by a Corinthian colonnade and pavilions and, inside this, a very large atrium gives a magnificent view of the façade. The immense five-aisled nave is imposing with its 80 granite columns supporting the arches and cornice and, over this, is a row of circular medallions each with its painted portrait. The windows above glow because of their alabaster filling but make the interior darker than it would be with glass. The ceiling is deeply panelled, coffered and richly carved. The great triumphal arch is covered by mosaic as is also the apse (**173**). The whole interior, though doubtless closely based on the original, as can be seen by Piranesi's eighteenth century drawings, has, however, none of the early Christian or Byzantine atmosphere of the other Rome or Ravenna churches. It is vast, cold, magnificent but artificial, its detail mechanical, its mosaics pre-Raphaelite in feeling.

S. Lorenzo-fuori-le-Mura, which was made up from combining two early Christian churches, one dating from 432 and the other 578, was partly destroyed in World War II and restored in 1949. The restoration has been excellently carried out and the interior retains its early Christian feeling, with the long nave, Ionic colonnade and timber roof. The floor is at a higher level in the sanctuary where it is built over the enormous crypt beneath. A smaller example, but one which retains its original character, is the church of *S. Sabina*,

The apse contained the altar in early Christian churches from the earliest days but this was not necessarily orientated towards the east.

EARLY CHRISTIAN CHURCHES IN ROME

171 Interior, S. Costanza, Rome, c. 340
172 Plan, S. Costanza
173 Interior, S. Paul-Without-the-Walls
    (S. Paulo fuori le Mura), 380. Rebuilt
    1823

171

172

173

built 425, with apsidal mosaics dating from 822 (**174**).

Apart from those on basilican lines, a number of early Christian churches were centrally planned and developed from the Roman mausoleum concept. A remarkably complete example is the mausoleum of Constantine's daughter, Constantina, now *S. Costanza*, built *c.* 320–50 next to the narthex of the cemetery of S. Agnese in Rome. This is on concentric, double circle plan, with central dome and sloping outer roofs. Inside the brick walls have niches, originally with mosaic covering. The circular colonnade has Composite coupled columns. The mosaics (now restored) cover the vaulted ambulatory (**171** and **172**). *S. Stefano Rotondo* is similar but has an inner ring of Ionic columns supporting an entablature while, across the circle, is a pierced dividing wall supported on two Corinthian columns. The outer walls are painted with frescoes.

The Byzantine Church

From the fifth century onwards the Byzantine forms of church plan were evolved from the Early Christian examples. *Basilican churches* continued to be built for a long time but many variations of form developed, with one dominant theme: a dome, or domes over an open space below. The chief characteristic of the Byzantine Church is the *dome*; it represented the symbol of the vault of heaven and its builders developed constructional ability in domical form which enabled them to create many different types of design with it as covering and architectural feature. In general, in the west the basilican plan prevailed, with Rome as inspiration, but further east, in Syria, Armenia, Greece and Serbia Byzantium acted as the model and the dome was the dominant feature.

The *exterior* of Byzantine churches is plain and simple; its appearance is ceded to the glory of the *interior*. The windows are small and the

174 Church of S. Sabina, Rome, A.D. 422–32

vital characteristic is the mosaic covering to all interior surfaces. These brilliant vitreous squares of colour catch the limited rays of light from the high windows of the drum and create a shimmering effect which glows and is alive in the semi-darkness of the church. These mosaics are not only decoration; they are an integral part of the Byzantine scheme of architecture. There are few columns or piers in these domed forms of construction, thus leaving open spaces in the interior where wall, vault and ceiling pictures can be seen without interruption. On these surfaces are depicted in gold and brilliant colour the story of Christianity. The mosaics effect the same purpose as the Gothic portals in the great cathedrals: they tell the Bible story to a population which could not read. There was a tradition for the placing of such mosaics. Generally the central dome which represented the vault of heaven was covered with a picture of Christ Pantocrator (the Ruler of All) surrounded by angels and His apostles. In the drum there were prophets; on the pendentives evangelists. Each part of the walls and the rest of the ceilings received their appointed section of the Christian story.

The chief types of *Byzantine church plan* are as follows:

1. The *domed basilica* where there is a central dome with an extension on the long axis into two semi-domes, e.g. Santa Sophia, Istanbul. This is a plan typical of Byzantium and its surrounding area.

2. *Cruciform plan* with dome over the crossing and often over each arm also, e.g. S. Mark, Venice.

3. The *domed hall church*: rectangular plan to building.

4. A *dome-over-square* church where each of the four sides of the square ends in an apse. This is an eastern plan, e.g. Armenia.

5. *Cross-domed basilica* where dome is extended by barrel vaults. Related to No. 1.

6. *Circular* or *polygonal plan* with dome in centre, e.g. S. Vitale, Ravenna.

7. *Cross-in-Square*. This is the classic Byzantine form, particularly of the second half of the period. There is a central dome rising on a drum which has a cylindrical interior and polygonal exterior. The drum is supported on a circle made by four pendentives

between four semi-circular arches which in turn are supported on four piers or columns. The church has a cruciform plan where, in western areas, the western arm is longer than the others. There are many examples of this form, mostly small. It is essentially Byzantine and was used particularly in Greece, Serbia, Sicily and Istanbul.

All these churches have domes which cover a central area and are supported on pendentives. The entrance is generally at the western end and, opposite on the other side, is an apse where the altar is housed in the sanctuary. The space between is the open naos or nave. There is generally a narthex at the western entrance, sometimes crowned by a dome or domes. There is no bell tower; these, as in Ravenna, were added later.

Architectural Construction and Building Materials

The outstanding contribution of Byzantine builders to architectural construction was, as we have emphasised, their development of the pendentive. The *dome* is the most typical feature of Byzantine architecture as were the orders to the Greek and the steeple to the Middle Ages. Without doubt the chief reason for this is the eastern influence on the Byzantine Empire. It is still disputed where exactly the dome based upon pendentives originated, but its adoption for use in Christian churches is now accepted as being from eastern influence not, as was originally thought, from Imperial Rome. The *essential characteristic of Byzantine dome construction* is that such a dome is supported upon and covers a *square* form. The Romans made only tentative essays into building such designs but in the eastern Mediterranean and even further east— in Persia, Iran, Armenia, Syria—Christianity had taken root earlier than in Rome and churches were built of this type from the second century A.D. onwards. Long before this time wooden huts were made in these areas, by primitive peoples, which had domed structures built over square forms supported by means of planks set across the angles of the square thus making it into an octagon. Certainly Byzantine domical construction was evolved from wooden prototypes, but from exactly which area of the Middle East and eastern Mediterranean is not established. Early Christian centres have been found in Syria, Alexandria, Anatolia and Persia, to name a few, and, while after the acceptance of Christianity as the official religion of the Roman Empire in 325, churches were freely built in Rome and the west; these generally had flat, timber roofs in basilican style. Contemporary churches in the eastern part of the Byzantine domains were domed with vaults of brick or stone and such domes covered a square plan.

To understand the nature of the difference between Roman dome construction and Byzantine and the development of the latter, a series of sketches are given on page 99 in Fig. **175**. 'A' shows the normal Roman approach to covering a space with a dome. This, as at the Pantheon in Rome, is to support the hemisphere upon cylindrical walls. Here no great constructional problems are created. Apart from this type of building, attempts had been made in many countries to provide an adequate base for the circular section of the dome so that it could be set upon a square section building. Such schemes were of one of the following types:

1. To place a flat slab of stone across each angle of the square thus providing an octagonal basis. This is a direct transference to stone or brick building of the primitive wooden hut method mentioned earlier.

2. Courses of stone were corbelled out from the angles of the walls of the square, each projecting beyond the others below and carried upon them. This is an advance but not suitable to carry a larger dome.

3. The *Squinch*. Here an arch or series of arches are flung across the angles in a similar manner to (2). This is stronger still. (See 'B' and 'C'). The squinch had been known for some time and was used in Persia, Turkestan, Armenia and Asia Minor. The earliest western examples are in the Mausoleum of the Palace of Diocletian at Split (now Cathedral) (**136**), the fifth century baptistery at Naples and in S. Vitale, Ravenna (**194**).

The Byzantine contribution was the *pendentive* and this is not only a more satisfactory solution but will support large domes. The earliest extant example is the immense dome of *S. Sophia* at *Istanbul*. The term 'pendentive' is to some extent

a misnomer since it appears to define a form which depends from the dome instead of, as it does, supporting it. In a pendentive method of construction the triangular spaces between the square section and the circular base of the hemisphere are built as if they are parts of a lower and larger dome so that their section is like that of an arch carried across the diagonal of the square space to be covered. This lower dome possesses a horizontal section which is concentric with the plan of the intended dome. As the lower dome is too large to fill the square space it is cut off in vertical planes formed by the four walls of the square. When the four remaining parts of the lower dome have been built high enough to form a complete circle within the walls of the square, this circle provides the basis for supporting the actual dome. The pendentive construction so far described is illustrated in Fig. **175** 'D' while in 'E' the dome is set in position above its lower dome (i.e. pendentives). Later, more complex constructions were built up further with a drum upon the pendentives, pierced by windows in the sides to light the building beneath, and the dome surmounted this drum ('F'). In pendentive construction the weight of the dome is transmitted via the four pendentives to the wall angles of the square and efficient abutment is needed at this point to offset the thrust. Given such abutment the construction is a stable and strong one. Such Byzantine domes are visible externally and are not obscured by timber roofing. Generally the dome roof is tiled.

Apart from the dome and pendentive construction, Byzantine methods and *materials* vary according to locality. In the main, building, particularly for churches, was in *brick*. This is true particularly of Greece, Italy, Egypt and southern Russia. *Stone* was, however, more common in southern France, Armenia, Georgia, Syria and on the Greek islands. In brick churches the whole construction was of this material, though interior wall facings, capitals and columns were of marble. On the exterior the brickwork was used for banding and in decorative patterns; bricks were laid at different angles in herringbone, chevron and fret patterns, for example. There are many fine Greek versions of this craft. Stone bands were also used to decorate the walls and arches. As in Roman times, the core of the walls was often concrete or rubble. White

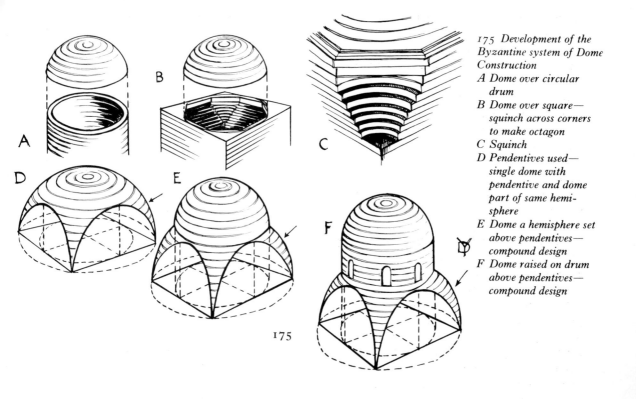

175 *Development of the Byzantine system of Dome Construction*
A *Dome over circular drum*
B *Dome over square—squinch across corners to make octagon*
C *Squinch*
D *Pendentives used—single dome with pendentive and dome part of same hemisphere*
E *Dome a hemisphere set above pendentives—compound design*
F *Dome raised on drum above pendentives—compound design*

175

Greek *marbles* were used for interior work also coloured ones from Thessaly and areas near Istanbul. In important buildings the interior decoration was by *mosaic* over all surfaces; in poorer churches painted *frescoes* were substituted.

Openings : Arcades, Doorways, Windows

Openings were either spanned by a semi-circular arch which rested directly upon the capitals, without entablature, or by a lintel. *Arcades* of semi-circular arches were used in churches to support galleries. *Doorways* commonly had semi-circular arches but alternatively flat, segmental or horseshoe designs (**183**). *Windows* were small, partly to keep the interior cool and partly to provide the maximum plain wall area for mosaic pictures. They had semi-circular arched heads and were generally filled with alabaster or marble sheets or, sometimes, glass. Many windows were single lights; others were two or three light designs. Most of them had pierced openings for part or the whole of the light, either left open or filled with glass (**180** and **181**).

Capitals and Columns

Byzantine capitals show great variety of form and detail. Classical capitals were interpreted, particularly the *Corinthian* and *Composite* designs, and in this form the wind-blown acanthus was a typical variation (**186**). Both *acanthus spinosus* and *mollis* plant forms were used. Such Corinthian capitals were adapted to Byzantine use; generally the two rows of acanthus leaves were retained but the rosettes and volutes were altered in different ways (**182**). Some capitals were based on the classical *Ionic* pattern but the volutes were much smaller (**176**). The most typical Byzantine form is the *basket* or *cubical* capital. These were decorated in many ways; with plaitwork, leaves, circles and geometric scrolls. Their chief characteristics were the deeply incised lines and drilled holes giving a strongly defined black and white effect (**177, 178, 179, 184, 185** and PLATES 29, 30). Many Byzantine capitals were surmounted by a *dosseret* (pulvino). This is a larger block set between the arch and the capital to provide a broader supporting top for the arcade above. Such dosserets are cushion or cubiform and are often carved with a cross in the centre of each face or by a monogram (**177, 179, 182, 184, 186** and PLATES 28, 29, 30). They were used in Greece and Italy but rarely in Istanbul. *Columns* were in early times taken from ruined Roman buildings. Later Byzantine columns were monolithic and usually of marble.

Ornament and Mouldings

Decoration was nearly all of an *applied character* and in the interior. The lower parts of the walls were generally panelled or veneered with slabs of marble in white and colours. The upper parts, the vaults and domes were covered by mosaic. There were few mouldings to interrupt this pattern and few corners or sharp edges. *Carving* was shallow and often only incised. It was employed on marble and was usually confined to capitals, pulpits and fonts. Figure sculpture was not permitted and motifs were chiefly in plant and geometrical form. A feature which often occurred comprised the cross and circle used in an interlaced ornament with acanthus or vine leaves. Deep, small holes were drilled at appropriate points in the leaf and stem decoration. The guilloche ornament was also used. All Byzantine decorative form is a mixture of east and west treated in a symbolic rather than realistic manner (**187**).

Mosaic

The covering of most of the internal wall and vault surfaces by glass mosaic was the predominant feature of Byzantine churches. In the dim light the gold and strong colours glittered and glowed with rich intensity. These mosaics have suffered great damage through the ages, particularly in countries occupied for centuries by the Turks such as Greece and Turkey itself. Mosaics have been whitewashed, damaged and destroyed in fires, earthquakes and wars. It is in *Ravenna* that the most accurate impression can be gained of how such interiors looked in the Byzantine era. Churches like *S. Vitale, S. Apollinare Nuovo* and, nearby, *S. Apollinare* in *Classe* have suffered damage and restoration but still present remarkable workmanship and much of their original splendour. In S. Vitale, in

particular, can be seen the typical combination of subjects in the Bible story depicted next to the Emperor Justinian, his Queen and his Court. The mosaics of the fifth and sixth centuries especially have a glowing richness of colour and a vividness of draughtmanship which complements their hierarchical treatment of figures and compositions. The simple drawing of figures and the conventional drapery are admirably adapted to this medium. Often the whole of the interior was covered in this way but the areas which received the most important designs and subjects were the dome, the apse, and the triumphal arch (PLATES 27, 31, 34, and 35).

Byzantium (Constantinople, or Istanbul)

In the fourth century A.D. Byzantium was a Greek city with connections with the Roman Empire. It had, indeed still has, a strategic position commanding the waters between east and west, between the Mediterranean and the Black Sea. It also had a good natural harbour and an established trade with the east and with Italy and France. The *Emperor Constantine*, impressed by the city's possibilities, transferred the Imperial seat of government there in A.D. 330 and began to build a great new city which he called New Rome. Later in the century the Roman Empire was divided into two parts, eastern and western, and after the fall of Rome in the following century, the eastern part ruled alone. Byzantium was renamed *Constantinople* after its first Christian Emperor and remained capital of a vast polyglot empire until its capitulation to Mohammedanism in 1453. Even before his death in 337, Constantine inaugurated many building schemes but, after him, one of the most famous names in building history of the empire is that of the *Emperor Justinian* who acceded in 527. He retook areas of land from the Goths and raised the empire to its greatest extent and power from Africa to Italy. He was also a reformer and builder; his reforms were far-reaching in administration and law while the arts flourished at a high level. He built fortifications, aqueducts, bridges, theatres and baths and planned whole cities. Many of his churches, which were numerous, still survive, particularly in *Istanbul* and *Ravenna*. In the mid-sixth century under Justinian the Byzantine Empire reached its zenith of influence and

Plate 27
Mosaic of S. George. Outer narthex, Church of
S. Saviour in Khora, Istanbul, Turkey, 13–14th
century
Plate 28 and Plate 29
Capitals, Poreć Cathedral, Yugoslavia, 535–43
Plate 30
Capital, Church of S. Vitale, Ravenna, Italy,
526–48

176 Capital. S. Sophia, Istanbul, Turkey
177 Capital. Poreč Cathedral, Yugoslavia
178 Capital. S. Sophia, Thessaloniki, Greece
179 Capital. Poreč Cathedral
180 Cupola. Church of the Holy Apostles, Thessaloniki
181 Cupola. Church of the Virgin, Stiris, Greece

182 Capital. S. Apollinare Nuovo, Ravenna, Italy
183 West doorway. S. Sophia, Thessaloniki
184 Capital. Poreč Cathedral
185 Capital. S. Mark's Cathedral, Venice
186 Capital. S. Sophia Cathedral, Thessaloniki
187 Perforated decorative panel. S. Vitale, Ravenna

greatness; it covered an approximate area of a million square miles.

The *city of Byzantium*, founded in 666 B.C. by the Dorian Greeks, situated on a hill above the Golden Horn, was too small to act as a capital city for the Roman Empire, so *Constantine* built new city walls enclosing a larger area. The new city, standing on seven hills and bounded by the Bosphorus and the Sea of Marmora, was easy to defend. It was laid out on Roman plan with six fora, the Imperial Palace, theatres, baths, hippodrome, etc. It was from this hippodrome that the four horses now on the façade of S. Mark's Cathedral in Venice were originally taken; they were set high above the track in Istanbul. Many churches were also built, after the adoption of Christianity, and *Justinian* in particular was responsible for the erection of the most famous of these. Between 410 and 1453 Constantine's *city walls* were extended to enclose a larger area and much of the walls still stand, encircling the city, as a monument to the importance of Constantinople during its 1123 years of rule as capital of the Christian Empire. There is an inner wall some 15 feet thick and an outer, thinner one. Towers were set at intervals and there was a terrace and deep moat. One of the main gateways was the *Porta Aurea* (golden gate), which was in marble in the form of a Roman triumphal arch with three archways and decorated with gilded sculpture.

Apart from these walls little remains today of the great Roman city laid out by Constantine and his successors. Warfare, which included the Crusades, and the neglect and decay since 1453 under Turkish rule, have destroyed the classical buildings and much of the ecclesiastical work. The churches were made into mosques and a number of these still stand, including the magnificent S. Sophia. During its years of power Constantinople was the largest city in Europe with a population of more than half a million. Arts, architecture and literature flourished and set a pattern for the whole of Europe. Its influence lasted in Western Europe and in Russia long after the collapse of the city.

S. Sophia 532–7

This great building is to Byzantine architecture what the Parthenon is to Greek. It was the proto-type of Byzantine pendentive construction for large buildings and, despite its later adaptation as a mosque and present use as a museum for tourists, the greatness has been preserved and, like the Parthenon, forms no anti-climax but creates a deep impression of its immensity and magnificence.

S. Sophia was built on the site of two earlier churches of the same name, one by Constantine in 335 and one by Theodosius in 415. After a disastrous fire the new church was begun by *Justinian* in 532 and was built in the incredibly short time of six years, though the interior decoration was completed after this. The architects were *Anthemius of Tralles* and *Isodorus of Miletus*. In plan the church is nearly a square; at the west end is the narthex and at the east the apse. There is a large central space of 107 feet square under the dome, which is supported upon four massive stone piers, while east and west of this dome are continued hemi-cycles which have semi-domes; these assist in containing the thrust and counter-thrust within the building itself. This construction creates a vast oval nave measuring 107 by 225 feet and it is the open space under this airy dome which gives the unique impression of light and floating architecture which is the chief quality of S. Sophia.

On the *exterior* the church measures 250 by 220 feet (**188** and **189**). On the north and south are enormous buttresses to take the thrust of the great pendentives and the main arches of the piers. These were built after the earthquake of 1305. The exterior view is somewhat disappointing and not easy of access. Like most Byzantine churches it is unpretentious and lacking in colour. The four Turkish minarets were added in the sixteenth century. At the west end is the great atrium which leads to the outer narthex (the marble columns of the atrium have disappeared). Through the triple entrance of the outer narthex is approached the main narthex which is constructed in two storeys. It measures some 205 by 30 feet and extends almost the whole width of the building. The upper storey is in the form of a gallery for women which extends into the church.

The *interior* of S. Sophia is monumental; the architectural design is simple but the effect dynamic in its quality of light and open space. The central dome is 180 feet above ground,

SANTA SOPHIA, ISTANBUL, 532-6

188 Plan
189 Exterior from the south-west
190 Interior, looking south-east

supported on gigantic pendentives* which in turn stem from the four semi-circular arches and enormous, ground-standing piers. The dome is made of brick with thick mortar joints. It is lighted by 40 small, arched windows which pierce the lower part. All the wall surfaces and the piers were faced with marble in white, green, blue, rose and black. The floors are in coloured mosaic with a gold background and with figures of apostles, saints and angels upon this. The columns are in coloured marble; the capitals, of white marble, are tremendously varied, some from ancient Roman temples, others Byzantine basket or cubiform designs. Originally they were gilded and had blue backgrounds. The domes and vaults were decorated with mosaic. The whole interior gives a feeling of weightlessness and harmony. The design is unique but has influenced many smaller churches. It has never been equalled on this scale. It represents one of man's great architectural feats and was technically a major step forward.

The mosaics of S. Sophia have been covered by layers of painted plaster over the centuries; in most places it is two inches thick. This is being removed slowly and carefully and, in the gallery in particular, one can see the glittering beautiful mosaic emerging from its years of cocooning, brilliant as ever, preserved by its coverings. In the nine-bay narthex, the mosaics are mainly plain gilt with crosses in the tympana, except the central one which depicts Christ. The quadrangular bays of the ceiling have formal floral designs in colour on gilt backgrounds.

From the ground floor of the church the viewer absorbs the impact of the immense church. Dominating the interior is the vast, shallow cupola supported on its tremendous pendentives and flanked by the half domes on the two long sides. The marbles are still rich and some of the mosaics are visible, but in general the colour is disappointingly dark and dull, showing little of the brilliance it once had.

From the gallery, one gains a clearer understanding of the plan and construction (190). The cupola and pendentives descend to the great flat sides, pierced by semi-circular headed windows and the arcades below. The two levels of arcades continue all round the church and the gallery, at first floor level, is of vast width and dimensions. The tremendous variety of capital

* These are the largest triangular pendentives in the world. Those at S. Peter's, Rome are of quadrangular form.

forms can clearly be discerned up here.

Since its original building S. Sophia has survived many dangers. It suffered damage by earthquake in the sixth century and in the tenth, the greatest deprivations and despoliation came from those who should be expected to respect it— the Crusaders. In the Fourth Crusade especially, in 1204, the interior was looted and the gold and treasure carried away to western Europe particularly to the Vatican in Rome. This despoliation was greater than any perpetrated after 1453 by the Turks who, in general, cared well for the structure and revered it as a mosque. S. Sophia remains the supreme achievement of sixth century Byzantine architecture.

Churches in Istanbul

Such churches had a western narthex through which a tri-portal entrance led into the building. The eastern end was commonly tri-apsidal. Walls were usually of stone while vaults and domes were in brick. In later churches there were many domes raised on drums. These examples were less cubical in basic plan and more elegant in design. Chief among surviving Byzantine churches are: *S. Saviour in Khora, S. Irene, SS. Sergius and Bacchus, S. Theodore* and *S. Mary Pammakaristos*.

S. Saviour in Khora

This church represents many Byzantine building periods. It was begun in 413 outside the city walls (hence its name, hôra meaning meadow). It was restored by Justinian and again enlarged and altered c. 1050. After damage in the Fourth Crusade it was further restored and added to in the fourteenth century (192). Some of the interior mosaics are of an early date but the majority, especially those in the narthex and domes, are of thirteenth century work and are very fine and rich. They represent today the finest mosaics in Istanbul and are quite as good a quality as those at Ravenna. Parts are missing owing to damage by fire and water, but the existing remains are beautifully displayed and in magnificent condition. Most of them are in the outer and inner narthices, on the walls, lunettes and in the ceiling shallow domes and ribbed cupolas. They are very detailed, made with small tesserae with gilt grounds and subtle colouring tones. The tech-

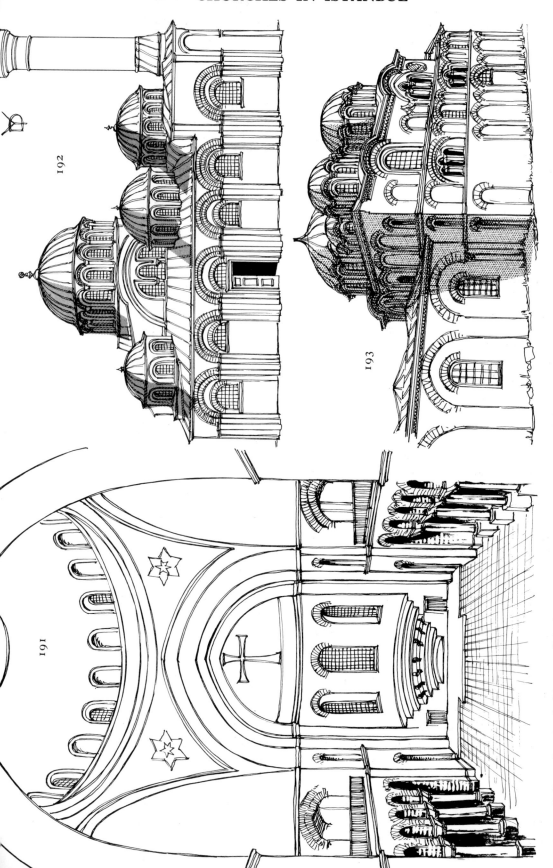

191 *S. Ireme. Interior, looking east. Begun 532*
192 *S. Saviour in Khora. Built before 413. Restored by Justinian in sixth century, and again in thirteenth century*
193 *S. Mary Pammakaristos, eleventh and fourteenth century*

nique is free and realistic for such an early date. They are pictorial, with good drapery and expressive features to the figures. The whole scheme tells the Bible story in considerable detail (PLATE 27). Originally the church had one dome raised on a tall drum but in later periods further domes were added so that now there are six. This tendency in later Byzantine work to add more domes in order to make the exterior more impressive is parallel to the Medieval desire to add spires to Gothic churches.

S. Irene

The church was begun in 532. The exterior still shows the original form well but has lost all decoration. The plan is that of a cross-domed basilica with nave, aisles, eastern apse and western atrium. The dome is one of the earliest examples raised on a drum and pierced with windows. The interior shows the basic form much as it was built, though it has been stripped of its decoration. There is a flattish central cupola and a secondary domical vault at the opposite end. The gallery (viewpoint of Fig. **191**), is arcaded in parts but solid in others.

SS. Sergius and Bacchus and Other Examples

This church is a classic example of the marriage between eastern and western Byzantine influences. It was built *c.* 527 by Justinian on a picturesque site on the shores of the Bosphorus. The construction is of Roman type, as is the masonry, but the decoration is Byzantine. In plan it is nearly square—109 by 92 feet. The exterior is uninteresting but the interior, now used as a mosque, is very fine. The central dome is vast. There are two storeys below it with a beautiful, rich, decoratively carved entablature on classical pattern and, below, Byzantine carved capitals of basket design and exceptional quality. Behind, in the ambulatory, are cubiform capitals of drilled hole type. The church is octagonal and has an apse on one face, opposite to the entrance.

Rebuilt in the twelfth century over a sixth century site the *Church of S. Theodore* is square in plan excluding a double narthex at one end and the *bema* at the other. It has five domes, the largest over the centre of the church and three are over the outer narthex; all are raised on high drums. The exterior is simple and typical of a small church; it is constructed of brick and stone in bands with coloured decoration and with arched window designs. The building is now a mosque. The minaret added to the present mosque is of brick and of a design to fit in with the rest of the church. The capitals in the wall arcade are bastard Composite and basket Byzantine.

The Church of S. Mary Pammakaristos (the All-Blessed Virgin) is a very fine late example mainly of the fourteenth century and is built on an interesting site overlooking the Golden Horn. It was converted into a mosque when the east end and dome were altered. The interior, especially the domed central space, is impressive. Part of the building is now used as a mosque and part as a museum. Only fragments of the mosaics remain but there are some interesting basket type leaf capitals surmounting the marble columns. The exterior is very like the Greek Byzantine churches, especially the examples in Thessaloniki (**193**).

The *Church of S. Saviour Pantocrator* (also later a mosque) is an unusual one in that it consists of three churches joined to one another and all of twelfth century date, but all have easy access to each other inside. Originally the decoration was in rich mosaic and marble but much of this has gone due to looting during the Fourth Crusade. The architecture is still in a fair condition and some of the marble facing remains.

The *Church of S. Theodora* originally belonged to a monastery; large cisterns found in the vicinity give credence to this theory. It is a small church, with an exo-narthex covered by three small domes. The mosaics here date from the thirteenth or fourteenth century. The church itself dates from the fifth century but was altered in the fourteenth century. The exterior capitals are interesting and varied.

The *Church of S. John the Baptist* belonged to the monastery of Constantine Lipos. It is a simple building with two domes or drums and a long façade. The building is low but extensive.

One of the most interesting early structures in Istanbul is not a church but the famous *cistern*, thought to have been designed by Anthemius of Tralles, one of the architects of S. Sophia. It is an underground cistern, still in fine condition and containing 336 columns mainly with Corinthian and cubiform capitals. The water level is lower than when it was in use but the level is sufficient to give reflections and provide an impression of what it was like. It was built in Justinian's day and measures 460 feet by 230. The ceiling is in brick, formed in groined vaults with barrel vaulted bays. The interior is now artificially lit and the appearance is impressive.

Italy and Sicily

Long before the fall of Rome Italy was suffering from barbarian attacks. The economy of the peninsula rapidly deteriorated and the seat of government of the western part of the Roman Empire was moved from Rome to different centres for safety. In A.D. 409 it was established at *Ravenna* and this area of the Adriatic coast from Ancona to the Istrian peninsula—designated the Ravennate—became the connecting link between Constantinople and the western half of its empire. Later in the fifth century Theodoric took over Ravenna as capital of the Ostrogothic kingdom but after his death in 526 Justinian recaptured the city and Byzantine control of the area was retained until *c.* 750. It is this part of Italy which today possesses the finest Byzantine architecture and art in the peninsula, in *Ravenna* itself, in *Venice* and the *Venetian Lagoon* and in *Istria*. In the south also Byzantine influence was strong from the seventh century until the Middle Ages. In *Apulia* and in *Sicily* the Saracens and Byzantine Greeks lived and worked, both giving to the region their style of architecture and high quality of craftmanship. Here Greek temples were adapted to become Byzantine churches— as at Syracuse (p. 21)—and new churches were built, particularly in Sicily.

Ravenna

The city of Ravenna was a naval port of Imperial Rome. Like Venice, it was built on a group of islands surrounded by marshes near the mouth of the river Po. Since that time the land has silted up in the river delta and the sea has retreated so the city, like Ostia, is now three to four miles inland. Because of the security of such a city the Emperor Honorius chose it as a refuge capital for the western part of the Roman Empire. Even today Ravenna is unique in the quality of its

Byzantine work, particularly the mosaics, most of it from the finest period of the fifth and sixth centuries. Some of the mosaics have been lost during the centuries but much remains and is carefully looked after by the Ravenna authorities.

There are three chief periods of work to be seen in Ravenna:

1. *The early fifth century*; the period when Honorius moved his capital from Rome (e.g. the Mausoleum of Galla Placidia and The Orthodox Baptistery).
2. *The Ostrogothic era*; Ravenna was taken by Theodoric in 493 and he ruled for over 30 years. He was a great builder and erected churches to the Arian religion (e.g. the Arian Baptistery and the Mausoleum of Theodoric).
3. *The Justinian era*; for over 200 years from 537 to the eighth century Ravenna was the seat of an Exarch, subject to Constantinople. The earlier part, under Justinian's influence, produced the finest work (e.g. S. Vitale).

Ravenna churches have a number of specific characteristics. They are Byzantine not Roman basilican. The eastern influence from Constantinople had merged with that of Italy to give a coherent style. They are built of red brick and are plain outside. The east end is apsidal, semicircular on the inside but, unlike the Roman, polygonal on the exterior; it is generally lit by three or five large windows. At the west end is the narthex and in later times a campanile has been added. Some examples have a baptistery near the church in the atrium. Inside, the columns are often from ruined Roman buildings but the capitals have been made specifically for the church and therefore the general interior scheme is more congruous than examples in Rome. The capitals, which are of varied Byzantine design, are superimposed by dosserets. The interior plan is commonly like the Roman basilican pattern with a timber roof and nave arcade of semicircular arches supported on columns, side aisles and mosaic decoration in the apse, triumphal arch and nave walls.

The Mausoleum of Galla Placidia, c. 430–40

This is a small cruciform building (33 by 39 feet), situated behind the church of S. Vitale, made of brick and covered by a central dome. The exterior is unpretentious but the interior is sumptuous. It is a very early example of both a cruciform construction and a dome upon pendentives and, because of its date, the dome and pendentives are part of the same hemisphere. The interior walls are lined with marble slabs and both dome and vaults still have their original mosaics which are of rich and exceptional quality. On the central part of the vault is a deep blue background decorated by stars arranged in concentric circles round a cross; at the corners are symbols of the four evangelists. In the lunettes are the apostles—figures in white and below, scenes from the Life of Our Lord. Particularly beautiful is the lunette of Christ as the Good Shepherd depicted as a young man seated with His sheep around Him. The lighting of this tiny interior is soft and gentle; it comes only through the alabaster panes of the small windows. Galla Placidia was the sister of the Emperor Honorius and died in Rome. This mausoleum was built to house her tomb but it is empty now.

The Tomb of Theodoric, c. 530

This original building which stands just outside the city was constructed by Theodoric, King of the Ostrogoths, as a mausoleum to house his ashes. It consists of two storeys and is decagonal in plan. The lower storey has thick walls while the upper one has thinner walls set back to form a terrace all round at first floor level. The upper part is circular, 30 feet in diameter, and is covered by a massive block of Istrian marble three feet thick and weighing 470 tons, which acts as a lid to the Mausoleum (**197**).

The Ravenna Churches

S. Vitale, 526–48

This is the most interesting and well preserved specimen of sixth century Byzantine church building in the west. The *exterior*, built of brick, is simple and plain but the interior is magnificent in its mosaic and marble decoration and its

unique capitals. S. Vitale was founded by Justinian. It is octagonal in plan, with a diameter of 115 feet. Inside this octagon is another, with a diameter of 55 feet, having an apse on each side of the figure except the east. The church had a narthex set at an oblique angle to one of the outer octagon sides; it is believed that this was not the original narthex, which would have directly faced the eastern apse (**195**). The inner octagon is covered by a dome supported on squinches which are made (which is uncommon) of small earthenware pots fitted into one another and are, therefore, light in weight. The dome is protected by a timber roof and is tiled on the exterior. The view from above in Fig. **194** illustrates the plan and construction of the building and shows the present entrance door on the left and the eastern apses on the right.

Inside the church, where the lighting is subdued but not dim, the central dome is supported on eight piers. It is now decorated by eighteenth century frescoes. There are, however, most beautiful *mosaics* of which the principal area is in the sanctuary. The apse mosaics have a gold background and are of early type, being stiff and formal in design. In the centre is the Saviour attended by two archangels. Below are the two famous panels; on the left is shown the Emperor Justinian and his court while on the right is the Empress Theodora with her attendants. Not only are these mosaics of great beauty and rich colour but they provide accurate data of the costume and appearance of Justinian's period and illustrate the hieratic splendour of the Byzantine court. In the centre of the vault of the choir is the crowning of the Lamb on a strong blue background and below this are four angels, and beyond, four evangelists. On the lunettes and walls are further panels representing scenes from the Old Testament. The *capitals* of S. Vitale are unusual and varied. They are surmounted by dosserets, decorated by animals and birds, and are mainly of cubiform or Corinthian design. They are of high quality, finely carved and are Byzantine in treatment with deep undercutting and drilling (PLATE 30).

S. Apollinare Nuovo, 526

The main interest of this church is in its *interior mosaics* because much of the building has been

Plate 32   Monastery of S. Luke of Stiris, Greece, tenth century

Plate 33   The Three Magi. Mosaic at S. Apollinare Nuovo, Ravenna, Italy, *temp*. Justinian

BYZANTINE ARCHITECTURE IN RAVENNA

194 *Church of S. Vitale, 526–47*

195 *Plan. S. Vitale. (Parts marked with dotted line do not now exist)*

196 *Church of S. Apollinare Nuovo, 493–525. Campanile sixth century. Portico Renaissance*

197 *Tomb of Theodoric, 530*

altered in later times. It was built originally by Theodoric, on basilican plan, as his Arian Cathedral. It was completed by Justinian and dedicated to S. Apollinare the first Bishop of Ravenna. The exterior façade, which is pleasant and striking, is now composed of the campanile *c.* 1000 and the sixteenth century Renaissance portico (**196**). Inside, the basilican plan is retained, with a flat, panelled timber roof decorated in gold and blue. There are high clerestory windows and nave arcade with simple Corinthian type capitals and plain dosserets above (**182**). The mosaics which cover the nave walls are of two periods; the upper pictures date from Theodoric's time and represent scenes from the Life of Christ and the figures of apostles and saints. Below these are the magnificent pageant panels of Justinian's time showing, on one side a procession of saints advancing towards Christ from the town of Ravenna (PLATE 35) and, on the other, virgin saints led by the Three Magi moving towards the Virgin from the port of Classis. The figures of the saints are dressed mainly in white and are shown against a gold background with palm trees in between. The Magi are in rich colours particularly red.

The *Church of S. John the Evangelist*, built *c.* 425, is on basilican plan and has one of the earliest of the Ravenna bell towers. This is on a square plan and dates from the ninth century. Unfortunately the church was severely damaged in an air raid in 1944 but has now been rebuilt to the original design. The campanile was largely spared.

S. Apollinare in Classe, 534–50

This church stands about three miles from Ravenna at *Classe* (Classis) which was the port for the city in the days of Imperial Rome. It was begun by Theodoric and finished in 549–50. It is a large, three-aisled basilica, 150 feet long and 98 feet wide, with a timber roof, nave arcade of semi-circular arches and a deep, high eastern apse which is circular on the inside and polygonal outside. The chancel is raised over a crypt below. The church is constructed of thin bricks with wide mortar joints; its atrium has disappeared but the narthex remains. On the north side is a very early, circular campanile, detached from the main church (**216**). Inside, the columns of the nave arcade are of marble and the capitals, with dosserets above, are typical—acanthus decoration with drilled holes pierced deeply. Unfortunately the church was despoiled of its marble wall covering in the fifteenth century when Alberti used it to enrich the Cathedral of Rimini. The mosaics in S. Apollinare are confined to the triumphal arch and the apse (PLATE 31). They make up in quality for their comparatively small area. In the conch of the apse is a great cross within a circle and with a background of stars. On either side are the figures of Moses and Elijah.

In Ravenna also are two interesting *baptisteries* with their mosaic decoration. They are both octagonal in exterior form and inside are decorated by mosaic pictures illustrating, in the dome, the Baptism of Christ. The finer of these is the *Orthodox Baptistery* built to serve the *Cathedral* in 449–52. The dome mosaic here shows the Baptism of Christ by S. John the Baptist; the background is gold and Christ is half immersed in water which, in the mosaic medium, has an unusual visual effect. In a larger circle round the central picture are apostles and saints against a dark blue background. There is a further circle and, beyond this, arches all round the baptistery in two tiers. The lower storey is richly ornamented in the arch spandrels with further mosaics in gold and blue with central figures and arabesque patterns around them. The arches are supported on columns with Composite capitals. There is a central font with marble floor around it. The other, the *Arian Baptistery*, is similar but plainer. It was built in Theodoric's time in *c.* 500. The mosaics are not so fine and are more hieratic.

The Ravennate: The Venetian Lagoon

Torcello

In the same manner and for the same reasons that Ravenna became the capital for the western part of the Roman Empire, the lagoons on the northern shore of the Adriatic became a refuge for people fleeing from barbarian attack. Communities which had fled from Rome and other cities established new centres of civilisation on these islands, which provided shelter and asylum from

ITALIAN BYZANTINE: THE RAVENNATE

the invader. One of the earliest of these settlements was on the island of Torcello on the Venetian Lagoon, and nearby Venice was established later. These new communities brought with them their tradition of culture and art and set up trading relations with Byzantium. The eastern capital, in turn, influenced the Venetian culture and the architectural form which developed here owes as much to Oriental bias as it does to Italy, particularly after the passage of two or three centuries.

Like Venice, *Torcello* was originally built on several islands and was a city with canal networks connecting these. Now it is only a small island with a few houses and the great cathedral with its accompanying church, S. Fosca. The *Cathedral of S. Maria Assunta* is a well-proportioned basilica with a tall campanile. It was built in the seventh century and after several restorations was finally reconstructed in 1008. Inside, the west wall is decorated by a mosaic representation of the Last Judgement. The capitals are all different versions on the Corinthian pattern and each has a double abacus, a straight sided one above and a curved one underneath; this is a later development from the dosseret and typical of Byzantine work of this date in Italy. The cathedral façade is decorated by tall, unbroken pilaster strips with blind arcading. A narthex extends across the façade and connects the cathedral to the neighbouring church of *S. Fosca* which is a small building with a portico which extends round the outside. This church was rebuilt in the twelfth century and is octagonal with an eastern apse (**198**). The buildings form an attractive group in contrasting Byzantine style and construction (**200**).

Aquileia and Grado

About halfway between Venice and the modern city of Trieste there is another island lagoon formation at Grado, where settlements were established at the same time as those in the Venetian lagoon. *Aquileia* was a Roman centre and the original basilican *cathedral* was erected early in the fourth century but was destroyed by Attila the Hun a few years later. Two basilicas were then built, side by side, the larger of which has disappeared. The other, after many restorations and additions, still exists and now has an eleventh century campanile and gabled west front with a low portico connecting this to the fifth century (roofless) baptistery. The interior is most interesting: it is large and has an 11-bay nave with varying classical capitals and columns. The mosaic pavement of the original church of c. 320 has now been laid bare; it is in magnificent condition and covers the whole of the nave and one aisle. Well illuminated, despite the tiny clerestory and aisle windows, the mosaic is in rich colours, particularly black and red, on a white background. The decorative scheme incorporates portrait Roman heads, animals, birds, fishes and Roman geometrical decorative forms. It is a wonderful example of a Roman Christian church pavement (PLATE 22).

Grado Cathedral, built on an island in the lagoon a few miles further south, is similar in design but the workmanship is not of such a high standard. It was founded in the fifth century and altered later. The atrium has gone, a campanile was added long afterwards and there is an early, octagonal baptistery at the north-east side (**199**). Inside, the original mosaic pavement of the sixth century is very fine and the twelfth century pulpit is of unusual design. The columns and capitals are from different buildings and do not match one another. The lighting is soft and pleasing due to the marble sheets in the windows (**201**).

Istria

The influence of the Ravenna school of Byzantine architecture extended further east along the Adriatic coastline and included the Istrian peninsula in what is now *Yugoslavia*. The *Cathedral of Parenzo* is an important example of this work. Now called *Poreč*, this cathedral was built in 535–43 and displays a high standard of design and craftmanship in its layout, carving and mosaic, all of which are well up to Ravenna standards and better than the work at Grado or Aquileia. The plan is that of a Roman basilica; in front of this is a covered atrium, finely preserved and with beautiful Byzantine capitals of varied form but high quality (**177** and **179**). In front of this again is an octagonal baptistery and further west still a later campanile. The eastern end of the church has an apse of Byzantine form, that is, semi-circular inside and polygonal outside. Originally the cathedral was decorated all

202 *Interior, Poreč Cathedral, Istria (Parenzo) 535–43,*
Baldacchino 1277.
203 *Plan, Poreč*

204 *Plan, Gračanicá*
205 *Church of the Virgin, Monastery of Studenica, 1183–91*
206 *Monastery Church, Gračanicá, 1321*

207 *The west façade, eleventh to fifteenth century.*
Domes thirteenth century
208 *Viewed from campanile showing Greek cross plan*
and siting of domes
209 *Plan*

ver, inside and out, with mosaic, stucco painting and inlay. Much of this has been preserved or restored, particularly the west front of the building, above the arcaded atrium, and inside. The exterior work is largely restored but the interior decoration in the apse is mainly original and consists of marble, porphyry and mother-of-pearl inlay on the lower part of the walls and mosaic above this and in the semi-dome. The nave has 10 bays and single aisles. The columns are of marble and have varied capitals of high standard—basket, Corinthian, Composite, and Romanesque types (**184** and PLATES 28 and 29). The walls are plain and there are small windows at clerestory level and in the aisles. A mosaic paving of an early floor has been excavated in two sections. It is like that at Aquileia but not so extensive or of such quality (**202** and **203**).

Venice

S. Mark's Cathedral : begun 1042

There are two buildings in Byzantine architecture which are of supreme importance constructionally and in design and which are also superb architecture. One is S. Sophia in Istanbul, the other is S. Mark in Venice. S. Sophia is the prototype and representative of the early period in Byzantine art—the sixth century—and S. Mark of the later—the eleventh century. S. Sophia represents the eastern approach to the architectural form, in Constantinople and S. Mark the western, in Venice. Yet, despite the five centuries which passed between the creation of these two buildings and their different geographical location, they have much in common. This is partly because the Byzantine architectural style altered comparatively little in its long history and partly because Venice is not a typical western European or even Italian city; its roots, owing to to its extensive commerce, are as much in the east as in the west. Both Constantinople and Venice were, between the sixth and fourteenth centuries, cosmopolitan cities and thriving commercial ports with wide connections with all nations of the Byzantine world from the western Mediterranean to Russia.

S. Mark's Cathedral is the third church on the site. The present building was begun in the mid-eleventh century and incorporates an earlier one which was partly destroyed by fire in 976. It was built as chapel to the nearby Doge's Palace and was made into the Cathedral of Venice in 1481. The plan is in the form of a Greek cross with arms of equal length and it is based upon the design of the famous Church of the Holy Apostles in Constantinople which had been begun by Constantine and rebuilt by Justinian but which was destroyed in 1463. S. Mark's Cathedral appears to be a complicated building, not easy to define, either from the façade in the great piazza or from the interior, and it is not easy to view from other aspects as buildings crowd closely upon it. The main reason for this is that the simple plan and elevation of the original cathedral have become obscured by later work, for the cathedral was being continuously added to, altered and developed from the eleventh to the sixteenth century. The *exterior* form is most clearly apparent when viewed from the campanile: a drawing of this view is given in Fig. **208**. The Greek cross plan is visibly marked by the five domes, one over the crossing and one over each arm of nave, choir and transepts. To the west of this is the great narthex with, behind, the complex façade of pinnacles, mosaic decoration and sculpture. It is a beautiful front but, as can be seen from above, it is only a façade, not a constructional form. The east end of the cathedral is apsidal (see plan, Fig. **209**).

The *west front* closes the eastern end of the Piazza S. Marco; this façade shows the rich and vital contrast between dazzling white marble and sombre coloured mosaic recesses. The lower part is the narthex with its five arches, all two-tiered and with relief decoration in the tympana. Mosaics cover the half-domes of the niches but only the extreme left doorway—the *Porta di Sant 'Alipio*—has its original mosaic of the thirteenth century; this illustrates the transportation of S. Mark's body to the new church and shows how the church looked at about 1210, based upon Justinian's Church of the Holy Apostles (PLATE 34). Many of the marble columns and capitals on this façade came from the earlier church and other Byzantine buildings in Italy and elsewhere (**185**). Above the narthex, set back, is the cathedral façade whose central window, now glazed, was originally traceried in marble. In front of this window are the four bronze horses taken from the Constantinople quadriga (p. 90). The five ogee arches of this stage of the cathedral are carved with white marble foliage, saints, angels and pinnacles and present a fretwork skyline; these are of Gothic workmanship. The façade is a complex mixture of styles and periods of work from the eleventh to sixteenth centuries, but it presents a coherent whole which is unsurpassed, even in Italy, for richness of colour and materials (**207**). The other elevations of the cathedral are also decorated with marble veneer, carving and mosaic. The south front was reconstructed as late as 1870.

The great *campanile*, over 300 feet in height, was built between the twelfth and sixteenth centuries. It collapsed in 1902 but was rebuilt to the same design. It is simple, decorated only with flat, low pilasters in brick, and has a belfry and pyramid above. It is in sympathetic contrast of plain verticality to the riotous curves of the cathedral façade.

The five *domes* of S. Mark's (**207** and **208**) have no drums. The central one is larger than the others; it is 42 feet in diameter and the other four are each 33 feet. Inside, the central dome rises nearly 100 feet above the cathedral floor. It is supported by massive piers at the crossing, each of which is 28 feet thick and is pierced by two tiers of arches, one at ground level and the other at the gallery stage. These piers support pendentives, like those at S. Sophia, which carry the dome. The other four domes are supported in a like manner and short barrel vaults connect one dome to another.

The *interior* is lit partly by the 16 windows in each dome which are set above the springing line, but this has been less effective since the thirteenth century when the outer cupolas were constructed. Now the interior lighting is not adequate and comes mainly from the west and transept windows and the small apse and aisle windows. Despite this deficiency the splendour of the interior is apparent. The whole scheme is covered by *mosaic* and *marble decoration*. The mosaics extend continuously over the surface of the vaults and domes and illustrate the Story of the Creation, the Fall of Man, the Legends of the Saints and the Miracles of Christ. These are of different dates—of which the earlier works are the best—but all have a gold background. The mosaic *pavement* is very fine while the *pala d'oro*, the golden screen in front of the high altar, is one of the glories of the cathedral. It was made, also

altered, between 976 and 1345 and represents on of the superb achievements of the goldsmith' and jeweller's art. There is a wealth of variety i the *capitals* in S. Mark's; most of these are of hig Byzantine standard of carving and design; ther are over 500 individual capitals in the cathedra (**185**). Some of the most beautiful mosaics are th thirteenth century pictures covering the vault o the great *narthex*. These represent over 100 scenes from the Old Testament; they have a gol background and are well lit. The great bronz *doors* of the central doorway, which lead from th narthex into the cathedral, were made in the earl twelfth century and are decorated in silver.

Sicily

Byzantine work in this area is of high standar and dates mainly from the eleventh and twelft century. It is, however, different in style from that of northern Italy due to the admixture o influences: Norman and Saracenic. The build ings are generally of solid, Norman constructio with Saracenic arcuated forms while the decora tion in mosaic, capitals, columns and carve ornament is a blend of Byzantine and Saracenic This combination of differing cultures creates surprising and most successful artistic form Most of the work extant is in *Palermo* and it surroundings. In the city itself is the Cappell Palatina and the churches of La Martorana, S Cataldo, and S. John of the Hermits while th nearby Cathedrals of Monreale and Cefal contain beautiful mosaics and carved marbl (see Volume 2).

The twelfth century *Cappella Palatina* (th Palatine Chapel) was the royal chapel of Kin Roger II and part of the Norman palace i *Palermo*. It is not a large interior but is superbl decorated. It has a nave of five bays with stilte Saracenic arches; the dome is supported o squinches and at the east end are three apses The entire interior surface is covered wit mosaic and marble decoration. The gold back ground and coloured pictures glitter and glow i the subdued light which filters through the tin round-headed windows and gives a sensation o unreality and fairy-like mysticism. The chapel i a fine illustration of the admirable blending o cultures: the construction and architectura design is Norman; the arches and carved stalactit

210 S. Cataldo, Palermo, Sicily, 1161
211 Church of Gorgeopekos, Athens (or S. Eleutherios or
The Little Metropole Cathedral), ninth-thirteenth century
212 Church of Kapnikarea, Athens, 875 and thirteenth
century

213 Plan, Church of Gorgeopekos
214 Plan, S. Cataldo
215 Church of S. Giovanni degli Eremiti (S. John of the
Hermits), 1132, Palermo

ceiling vaulting are Saracenic; the mosaic is Byzantine. These mosaics stem from different periods; the earlier ones by Byzantine Greek craftsmen are the finest, the later Italian ones are less rich and vital.

The *Church of La Martorana* in *Palermo* originally belonged to the monastery of that name. It now stands alone and has a baroque façade is plain also, while the east end is apsidal Byzantine dome and drum with beautiful mosaic decoration on a gold background. The adjacent campanile is also interesting and is a combination of Norman and Byzantine work. Next door to La Martorana is the *Church of S. Cataldo*, built in 1161. It has typical Sicilian plain domes, three of them in a row, and a Saracenic parapet. The façade is plain also while the east end is apsidal (**210** and **214**). The interior is simple and has now hardly any painting or mosaic except on the floor. The three domes have deep drums and light the church by small, round-headed windows, pierced in Byzantine fashion with round holes. The capitals are Corinthian except for one which is in Romanesque animal form. It is a charming Norman interior reminiscent of S. John's Chapel in the Tower of London but also has an affinity with the small Byzantine churches of Greece.

Also built by the Normans in 1132–48 but containing Byzantine and Saracenic craftmanship is the *Church of S. Giovanni degli Eremiti* (S. John of the Hermits). The exterior has plain golden-coloured walls, a campanile and five, red simple domes like those at S. Cataldo. Each bay of the nave is covered by domes and there are further domes over the choir, south transept and north transept bell tower. Like many Sicilian buildings the windows are very small so as to exclude the hot sunshine (**215**).

Byzantine Influence in Southern France and Northern Italy

In these areas there exist a number of churches which are Byzantine in inspiration but which differ from the eastern pattern in their execution. They are buildings of the Romanesque or Gothic periods and possess strong Byzantine characteristics. In *France*, the region formerly called *Aquitaine* is principally where such churches are to be found, particularly in or near Périgueux (Dordogne in modern France). Here, the major

example is the *Cathedral of S. Front* in the town of Périgueux. Originally a Benedictine Abbey Church, which was destroyed by fire in 1120, it was rebuilt soon after this much on the pattern of S. Mark's in Venice and was made into a Cathedral in 1649. Like S. Mark, the cathedral is based on the Greek cross plan and has five domes, one over each arm and one over the crossing. These domes are carried on pendentives and are each 40 feet in diameter. The light to the interior of the Cathedral is low due to being provided mainly by four tiny windows in each dome. Also like S. Mark's, the domes are supported on massive square piers which are pierced at two levels by round arched passages. However, there are some differences between this western version and eastern Byzantine large churches. The domes are not hemispherical but spheroidal in shape and are elongated towards the top; the pendentives are also elongated and more in the form of squinches. In the late nineteenth century the cathedral was extensively restored and altered, particularly the main apse which is now disproportionately large, but much of the twelfth century work remains, especially inside. S. Front is similar in size to S. Mark but the workmanship is not so fine (**218, 219** and **220**). Other churches in the area which have similar Byzantine characteristics also differ mainly from the Constantinople pattern by their ovoid domes, elongated and double curved pendentives, their Romanesque fenestration and arcading; also these churches are built on the western style Latin cross plan. Such examples include the *village church* of *Tremolat* (Dordogne), that at *Paussac*, near Bourdeilles and the *church* at the village of *Brassac-le-Grand*. All these have several domes carried on pendentives and were built between the eleventh and thirteenth centuries.

South-west France, which was much further from the central sphere of Byzantine influence, showed, through trade influence, more evidence of church designs of this type than *northern Italy*, which was much nearer. There are, however, one or two examples and the chief of these is the basilica of *S. Antonio* in *Padua* (1232–1307). This is a large, pilgrimage church, also reminiscent of S. Mark's in Venice. The exterior is very fine and all the seven domes are visible; at the east end is an apse with chevet and nine radiating chapels; the west front has an upper, arcaded

BYZANTINE ARCHITECTURE IN FRANCE AND ITALY

216 *S. Apollinare in Classe, nr. Ravenna, Italy, 534–9*
217 *Basilica of S. Antonio, Padua, Italy, from the north-west, 1232–1307, 7 domes*
218 *Cathedral of S. Front, Périgueux, France, interior 1120–50*
219 *Cathedral of S. Front from the south*
220 *Plan of Cathedral of S. Front*

BYZANTINE CHURCHES IN THESSALONIKI (SALONICA) GREECE

221 *Church of the Holy Apostles, c. 1315*
222 *Church of Our Lady of the Coppersmiths (Chalkaion), eleventh century*
223 *Interior of Rotunda of the Emperor Galerius c. 310. Made into Church of S. George fifth century*
224 *Plan*
225 *Exterior of the Rotunda*

gallery of pointed arches. Inside, the nave is in square bays which are covered by domes on pendentives. The other domes cover the crossing, choir and transepts. The general interior layout is magnificent, but later alterations have made the decoration of a lower standard. Most of the interior dome surface is now plain (**217**).

Greece

There are a large number of *Byzantine churches* in Greece especially in *Thessaloniki, Athens*, the area near *Delphi* and in the *Peloponnese*. They are of characteristic design and differ from those in other Byzantine regions. They are less ornate than those in Serbia and smaller and simpler than those in Constantinople. They are nearly all of the late Byzantine building period—eleventh to fourteenth centuries—and mostly have many domes raised on drums. The maximum possible wall and vault area inside is covered by mosaic or, in poorer churches, by fresco paintings. Most designs are based on the cross-in-square plan and have an apsidal east end, generally with three apses of which the centre one is larger and contains the altar. At the west end the narthex is commonly enclosed as part of the church which thus resembles a square in plan. Most of the churches are small.

Thessaloniki (Salonica)

Of all *Greek cities* this one was the most important under the Byzantine Empire and shows the closest affinity in art and architecture with Constantinople. In the later period, from the tenth century, it was the second largest city of the empire and its rich Byzantine heritage still shows this.

Cathedral of S. Sophia

This is one of the largest and earliest of Greek Byzantine churches. The exact date of its original building is disputed but it probably stems from the late fifth or early sixth century. It has been considerably altered, mainly under Turkish rule, and then later restored so that the exterior, in particular, is changed. It is a domed basilica with a tri-apsidal east end, a wide western narthex which runs round three sides of the church like S. Mark's Venice, and a central dome, 45 feet in diameter, carried on pendentives. Some very fine original mosaics remain. In the dome is represented the Ascension with Christ seated on a rainbow and surrounded by a ring of angels and apostles alternating with olive trees. In the apse is an earlier mosaic—about eighth century—showing the Virgin and Child (**178, 183** and **186**).

Church of S. George, c. 310 onwards

This is an unusual building with a chequered history, having served as Roman temple, Christian church and Mohammedan mosque. Now, almost empty, it is a museum. It was built *c.* 310 as a Roman rotunda by the Emperor Galerius and, like the Pantheon, has eight great arches and entrances on the ground floor and a massive dome overhead. It is lighted by semi-circular headed windows above these. The dome, 80 feet in diameter, is based, Roman fashion, on walls of cylindrical plan which are 20 feet thick to support it. In the fifth century it was converted into the Church of S. George and the dome decorated by mosaics, few of which remain. The dome was covered on the outside by a flattish pitched roof, an ambulatory was constructed round the rotunda which became the nave and a chancel was added at the east side. The minaret is a souvenir from the Turks' use of the building as a mosque. In its present form it is more like the original Roman Pantheon and is a most interesting example of Roman brick arcuated construction (**223, 224** and **225**).

Church of the Holy Apostles, 1312–15

Situated on the hillside which rises above the port of modern Thessaloniki the Church of the Holy Apostles is not easy to find amidst the poorer districts of the town, but it is well worth the effort of searching. The exterior, especially, is a perfect example of its type in good condition. It stands in a small square, now some five feet below the present ground level, surrounded by cypress trees. The Turkish buildings which had adjoined its walls have now been removed and the church can be seen clearly. It is made of polychrome brick in richly decorated patterns in reds, browns and yellows. It has five domes on high drums with projecting cornices on each of their sides. The high quality of the brickwork is unique in the typical late Byzantine patterns of zig-zags, frets and diamonds (**180** and **221**). The interior has suffered seriously at Turkish hands and the frescoes have been badly damaged.

Church of S. Demetrius, late fifth century

This was one of the finest and largest churches here but, having survived much of the bombardment of the First World War, it was seriously damaged in the fire of 1917 when its wooden roof was totally destroyed and caused great ruination when it collapsed into the church. Now the building has been restored but with newer and different materials, mainly white marble and red brick. Only a few capitals and a little of the marble panelling and mosaic remain of the original decoration. These have been preserved and incorporated into the new, impressive church.

Athens

A number of churches here survived the Turkish occupation, but were lost in the nineteenth century when the capital of the newly independent Greece was re-organised and planned on broad lines. Those remaining include the *Church of Gorgeopekos*, the *Kapnikarea, S. Nicodemus* and *S. Theodore*.

The first of these, the *Church of the Virgin Gorgeopekos* (also called S. Eleutherios or the Little Metropole Cathedral due to its proximity to the great nineteenth century Metropolitan Cathedral) is the most interesting. It is a tiny building, only 38 by 25 feet, and now stands a little below the present pavement level. It has a central dome, nine feet in diameter, on a high drum pierced by small windows, which is supported on four piers. The church is built of white Pentelic marble and is decorated by sculptured slabs and panels mainly of decorated marble taken from other buildings, thus illustrating a mixture of Greek classical and early Byzantine work from egg and dart carving to signs of the zodiac and dragons (**211** and **213**). The *Church of the Kapnikarea*, built originally c. 875 and enlarged in the thirteenth century, now stands on a small island in the centre of Athens traffic.

It is of similar plan to the Little Cathedral but is larger; at the east end are three polygonal apses and there is a beautiful thirteenth century porch. The central dome is small—only six feet in diameter—and is decorated inside with gold mosaic (**212**).

The other two churches are less interesting due to alterations and restorations in later periods. *S. Theodore,* c. 1065, is situated in a pleasant square. It is built on Greek cross plan and has a small dome on an octagonal drum. It is of stone with thin bricks between. The east end is apsidal with three polygonal apses and there is a later bell tower at the south side. *S. Nicodemus* is the oldest of this group of churches but was excessively restored and altered in the nineteenth century when the campanile was built.

Monastery Churches

Daphni

Here is an eleventh century monastery church situated in a grove by the side of what was originally the sacred way from Eleusis to Athens (now a dusty highway with commercial traffic pounding from modern industrial Eleusis to the capital's port at Piraeus). The fine Byzantine church was considerably restored in the nineteenth century, but retains its original character. It is built of sandstone with red bricks set between courses. The east end has the three polygonal apses, the central one taller and larger, and the dome rises above an eight-sided drum and is capped by a flattish, tiled roof. Inside, the mosaics and frescoes are very fine especially those of the dome which illustrate the Christ Pantocrator in all His Glory (**229** and **230**).

S. Luke of Stiris (Osios Lukas)

The monastery buildings here are in a beautiful mountain setting between Levadia and Delphi where peace and solitude still remain, tourists apart. Architecturally the buildings form an unusual and interesting group consisting primarily of two churches joined together; the larger S. Luke and smaller church of the Virgin (**226** and **228**). The monastery takes the form of an open square in which the two churches stand. The *Church of S. Luke* has a central dome carried on 12 piers with squinches to transform the

BYZANTINE CHURCHES IN GREECE

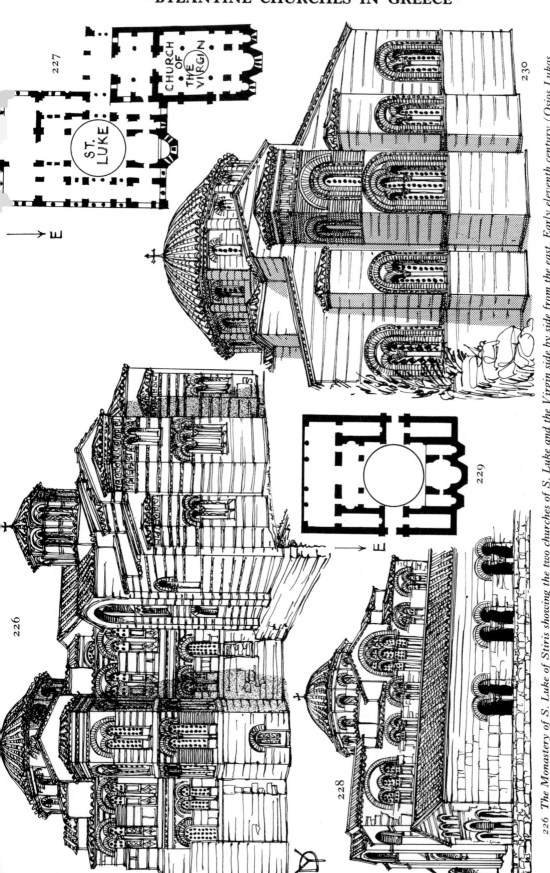

226 The Monastery of S. Luke of Stiris showing the two churches of S. Luke and the Virgin side by side from the east. Early eleventh century (Osios Lukas, near Delphi)

227 Plan of the two churches

228 Church of S. Luke from the south

229 Plan. Monastery Church of Daphni, ninth century

230 Monastery Church at Daphni from the east

square into an octagon while higher up are small pendentives which convert the octagon to a circle. The rest of the church is vaulted and the vaults, dome, squinches and walls are richly decorated with coloured marble and mosaic. The dome is raised on a drum which has 16 windows (some now walled up) while each arm of the cross has a half-dome. The east end is apsidal with a single polygonal apse. The mosaics in the narthex are in good condition, restored, in brilliant gold and colours. The floors throughout are of the original coloured marble while large portions of the windows still possess their original marble slabs. The smaller adjoining *Church* dedicated to *the Virgin* is also eleventh century and has a fine dome on an octagonal drum which is pierced by double windows which have slender, marble shafts between the lights. Between the windows the drum is richly panelled in carved marble slabs (**181**). Like the Church of S. Luke, the floor is of beautiful coloured marble and the walls and vaults are decorated by marble and mosaic. The eastern end is tri-apsidal, polygonal on the exterior (**226**).

Mount Hymettos

There have been several monasteries here on the mountain slopes above the city of *Athens*; they are now deserted and partly ruined. The largest of them is the *Monastery of Kaisarani*, which has a beautiful situation surrounded by cypress trees. The church dates from the eleventh century and is magnificently decorated by fresco paintings in the narthex, dome, apse and on the walls. The dome is supported on four columns which have Ionic capitals taken from a classical temple which earlier stood upon the site. Higher up the mountainside is another, smaller church of the *Monastery of Asteri* which is equally finely situated and has magnificent views of the hills encircling Athens and of Daphni.

Meteora

In these remote valleys of *Thessaly*, not far from the city of Larisa, are the remains of some of the most remarkable monastery churches. Originally, in the fourteenth century, there were 30 monasteries, now, only five or six remain. The churches are small, perched on the summits of

high, needle-like rocks which rise sharply from the valley floor and in which the monks lived and prayed in retreat from the world at large. Two of the most impressive survivors of these churches are those of the *monasteries* of *S. Barlaam* and *S. Stephen*. They are built on the Byzantine pattern, in small scale, and have painted fresco decoration.

Mistra

Much further south, near ancient Sparta in the *Peloponnese*, is the now deserted city of Mistra (Mystras). On a rocky hill, about 2000 feet above the sea, Mistra was developed in the late days of the empire from the fourteenth century and was, at that time, an important centre and therefore contained some large churches. Most of these are now desolate except for the fifteenth century *Church of the Pantanassa*, still a convent, and a few others such as the fourteenth century *Church of Evangelistria*, *S. Sophia*, *c.* 1350, and the fourteenth century *Church of Peribleptos*. The Church of the Pantanassa is particularly fine, sited on a hillside ledge overlooking the valley. It has five domes on drums and a belfry, also a loggia. Inside, there are frescoes in rich colour typical of the best of late Byzantine work. There were also a number of outstanding secular buildings such as the *Palace* with its great hall and courtyard, but much of the rest of the city is in ruins.

Asia Minor

Christianity spread here early and into Armenia and Georgia. Many churches were built but almost all are ruined or have disappeared. A number of examples were domed basilicas, particularly on the coast, while inland churches were small and of stone, usually with barrel vaulting. An important church is that of *Khodja Kalessi*, built *c.* 451, in *Southern Turkey* in the ancient region of Cilicia, but this is partly ruined. Remains of many churches still exist in and near the ancient city of *Ephesus* (Efes). The most notable are those dedicated to S. Mary and to S. John. S. Mary, the cathedral where the Council of Ephesus met in A.D. 431, is sometimes referred to as the 'Double Church' because of its different building periods. Only fragments remain

RUMANIAN AND BULGARIAN MONASTERIES AND CHURCHES

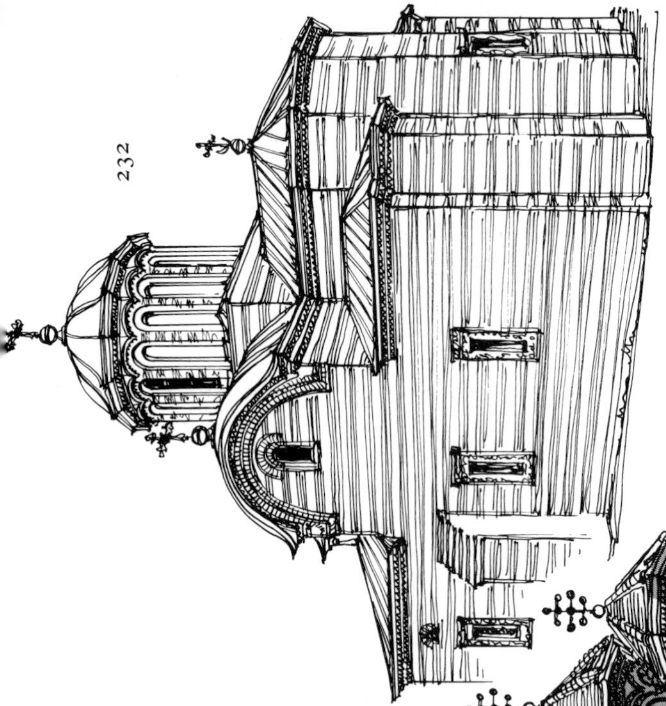

231 Cozia Monastery,
Olt Valley, Rumania,
1387–8
232 Church of S.
Nicholas, Curtea de
Arges, Rumania, c. 1330
233 Fourth century
Church of S. George,
built on site of Roman
Bath. Now in courtyard
of Hotel Balkan, Sofia,
Bulgaria
234 Snagov Monastery
Church. Built on island
in Lake Snagov,
Rumania, 1517

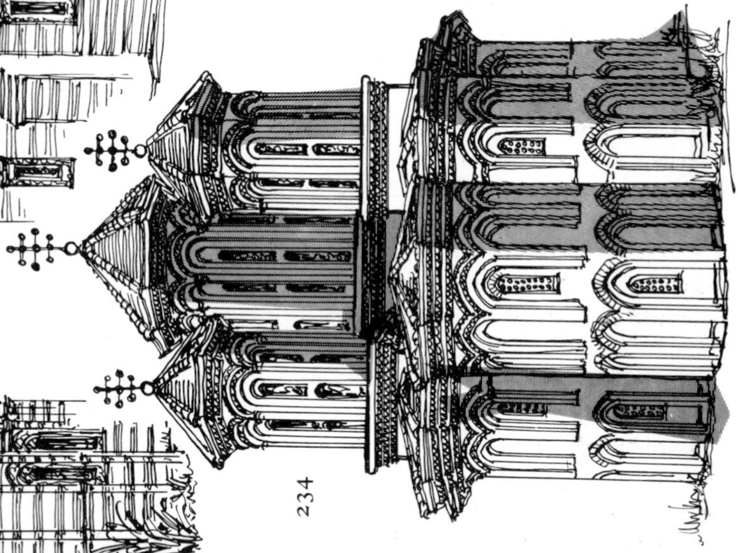

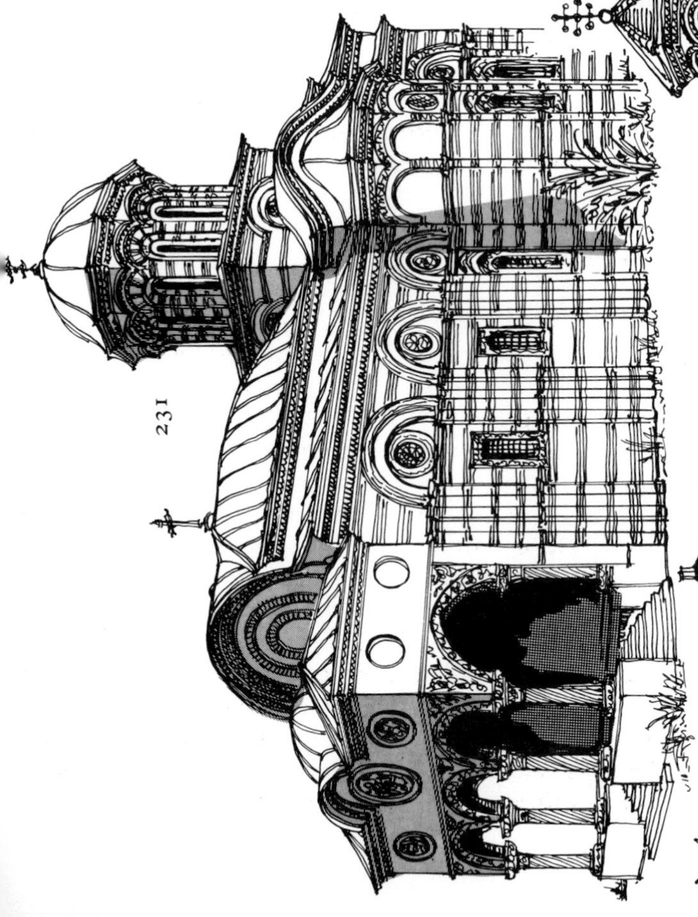

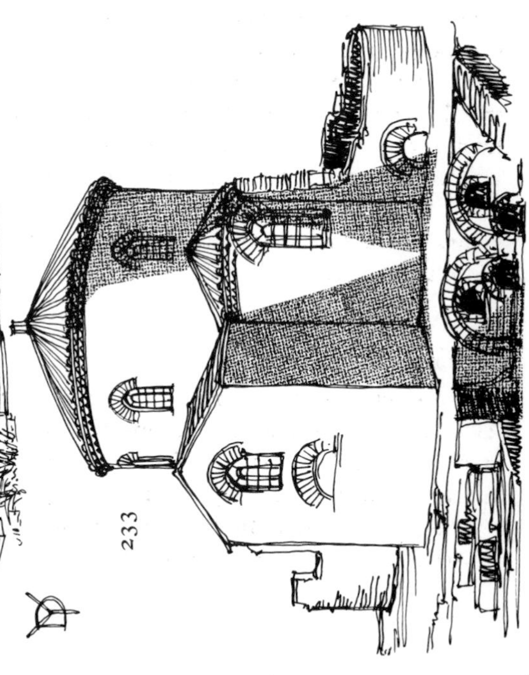

232

234

231

233

but these show the immense size of the building, over 400 feet in length. The church of S. John was built in the early fifth century then re-built by Justinian about 565. This was a famous and magnificent building but only a small, well preserved, portion remains.

Armenia

Armenian Byzantine churches have something in common with Greek designs and date chiefly from the tenth to the thirteenth century. Those of the tenth century are the finest and richest. The churches are small in plan but tall in proportion. Ground plans are square or rectangular and the east end is apsidal, generally with three polygonal apses which are semi-circular inside. The domes are constructed on high drums but are hidden externally by steep conical, stone roofs. The most famous example is the *Cathedral* at *Ani*, the capital, now called Erivan (Yerevan) and under the jurisdiction of the U.S.S.R. This cathedral dates from 1010 and is of cross-in-square design but with longer east and west arms. It is in a ruined condition.

Yugoslavia

Many interesting examples of Byzantine work have survived in the territory which comprises modern Yugoslavia and they stem from either Italian or Serbian origins. The northern part of the Adriatic coast was under Italian influence, of which the best example is *Poreč* (Parenzo) already described on pp. 116, 119 (**202, 203**), while the mountainous central area extending as far as the southern part of the Adriatic coastline contains Serbian Byzantine churches. These are a relic of the independent existence of Medieval Serbia when this territory was of great importance in the Balkan Peninsula at a time when the Byzantine Empire was at a low ebb. For over 200 years, in the late Byzantine period, Serbia was strong and influential and built many monasteries and churches before succumbing to the Ottoman Empire. In architectural style these churches are generally tall, like the Armenian ones, but very richly decorated in brick and stone. They have numerous domes on tall drums. The surviving examples are almost all in or near tiny villages in remote mountain regions; among the

best are those at *Studenica, Dečane, Gračanica* and *Kruševac*.

The *monastic royal Church of Studenica* was built beside a river of the same name in 1183 in the central mountain area far from any large town, the nearest being Niš (**205**). Its walls are faced with white marble and the interior is richly decorated with fresco painting. The *Monastery of Dečane* is south of Studenica, in even wilder country near the Albanian border. It was built in the fourteenth century and shows Italian influence, being designed by craftsmen from Kotor (Cattaro) on the coast south of Dubrovnik where there is further Byzantine work. This Italian feeling is shown in the decorative bands of black and white marble and sculptured tympana which are Romanesque in type. However, the dome, general plan and interior frescoes are Serbian Byzantine. The *Church* at *Gračanica*, built 1321, is one of the most striking examples of Serbian Byzantine architecture. In the mountains not far from Dečane and near the present-day town of Prština, it lies just off the main road to Skopje. It has a tall central dome and smaller ones, also set on drums, over the angle spaces. The exterior has a fine, grouped massing of domes typical of the late Byzantine period and the brick decoration is rich and of high standard. Inside are fresco paintings (**204** and **206**). The *Monastery Church at Kruševac* is near to Studenica and part way between Niš and Belgrade. It is also a fourteenth century church and shows Romanesque tendencies in its sculptural decoration.

Rumania and Bulgaria

Like Russian Byzantine architecture, the best *Rumanian* Byzantine churches belong to a late period, in some cases, after the collapse of the Empire in Constantinople. In style, however, they are more usually like those of Serbia.

One earlier example is of the cross-in-square type with a dome over the crossing. This, the *Church of S. Nicholas* at *Curtea de Arges*, has a poly-sided drum. The exterior is built in simple brick and stone courses and, like the interior has been restored a number of times. Inside the decoration is remarkable. All surfaces—dome, drum, pillars, chancel screen and walls are covered in paintings, some of which belong to the fourteenth century building period (**232**).

RUMANIAN CATHEDRALS

235 *Patriarchal Cathedral, Bucharest. From the south-west, seventeenth century*

236 *Cathedral and royal mausoleum, Curtea de Arges. From the south-east, Early sixteenth century*

236

235

The more common Rumanian pattern is on trefoil plan with a square narthex at the west end. *Cozia Monastery Church* is an example of this design (**231**), with a dome over the central part. Traditionally Byzantine in the building materials and plan, it is more eastern in the decoration and treatment. The monastery has a beautiful situation, on the very edge of the river Olt in fine mountain country. The interior has painted surfaces all over; especially interesting are those in the narthex.

Two famous churches of early sixteenth century date are the *Cathedral of Curtea de Arges* and the *Monastery at Snagov*. The Cathedral is a remarkable building, richly ornamented inside and out. The exterior gleams in gold and colour and stands in a park amidst beautifully kept flower beds. It was built in 1517 as a royal mausoleum. The tombs are in the narthex which is large, almost half the building, and which is approached by a flight of steps. One large dome and two smaller ones with twisted columned drums are set over the narthex which has 12 columns to support them inside. The main church behind is small and high, with the largest dome over it. This building is on the typical Rumanian trefoil plan, with three apses round the square (**236**). The intricate decoration shows a variety of motifs and designs from Byzantine, Renaissance and Mohammedan sources. There are no mosaics inside but paintings on all surfaces. The columns are ornamented in geometrical designs but on the apses, domes and walls are depicted biblical scenes with the Christ Pantacrator, apostles and saints.

Snagov Monastery occupies a romantic and peaceful island site in the Lake of Snagov which is now a centre for boating, fishing and bathing, used at weekends and holidays for the city dwellers of near-by Bucharest. The monastery church is small and lofty, on cinquefoil plan and with four drums and domes very like their Serbian counterparts. One large dome covers the crossing, another the narthex and there are two smaller ones over the eastern apses (**234**). The church is built of brick (recently restored) and has narrow slit Byzantine windows. Inside four arches support the central dome with squinches rather than pendentives. Below the arches are fat, circular columns instead of the usual piers, and there are openings between these and the apses. The chancel is barrel vaulted. The interior surfaces are painted with work dating mainly from 1815.

The Byzantine style of church building continued, as in Russia, for several centuries. Later, larger buildings were more complex in plan and construction with a multiplicity of domes but, often, basically on cross-in-square foundation. The *royal church* at *Tîrgovişte* not far from Curtea de Arges is one of these, built in the sixteenth century. Similar, but larger, is the *Patriarchal Cathedral* at *Bucharest*—dating from the seventeenth century and several times restored (**235**). This has a fine site, surmounting a hill in a park overlooking the busy, central Piata Unirii. The building has a large narthex extending the whole width of the church with three saucer domes over it. These and the walls are painted all over. The eastern end of the Cathedral is tri-apsidal and there are four domes on tall decorative drums.

Bulgaria also had a long history of Byzantine building of churches and monasteries but remains of original work are not numerous or of high quality. Earthquakes took a high toll, as at Turnovo, and some of the more famous examples, like Rila Monastery, near Sofia, have been rebuilt much later (see Volume 4).

Serbian influence was strong in Bulgaria, as in the Turnovo churches, but more common were the aisleless halls, barrel vaulted and with two domes raised on drums, one over the centre and one the narthex. S. Dimitri at Turnovo was one of these.

Among the work still surviving is the *Monastery* of *Bachkovo*, near Plovdiv, which was built in 1083. Its early seventeenth century church is pleasing and interesting. *Rozhen Monastery*, near Melnik, is of early date. The Church of the Holy Virgin in the courtyard is of the fourteenth century and contains some fine wall paintings.

Most dramatically situated is the *Preobrazhensky Monastery*, near Turnovo. It is lodged on a shelf on the mountain gorge, high above the Yantra river with precipitous rocks falling steeply below it. The long, low church is decorated by paintings all over the exterior and interior walls, openings and window frames. The roof is tiled and the cupola is of Greek Byzantine type. The monastic buildings surround the church and spread up the hillside above. Inside, the church is designed in three parts. The centre portion is the largest and is surmounted by the shallow cupola on an octagonal drum carried on squinches with four arches below. The naos has a painted barrel vault and the pro-naos a flat-timber roof. The paintings are all of biblical scenes with Russian Byzantine influence.

Russia

The Byzantine origins and influence dominated much of Russian architecture even into the sixteenth and seventeenth century. The Russians were interested in and finally converted to Christianity at the end of the tenth century and from this time onwards their ecclesiastical architecture was based on that of Constantinople while the churches were, in many cases, built and decorated by Byzantine craftsmen. After the collapse of the Byzantine capital it continued as inspiration for Russian architects and artists who gradually adapted the style to their own climate, building materials and taste. This was particularly so in the area round *Novgorod*, where the dome was altered to Russian designs and climatic needs and established the characteristic Russian church skyline. By the twelfth century the typical onion shape had emerged whereby the dome was increased in diameter above the springing then became more slender and steep above to throw off the rain and snow. The number of domes used increased and larger buildings had many, all on cylindrical drums and placed almost haphazardly on the building. The results were striking, especially when bright colour decoration was added as in the *Cathedral of S. Basil in Moscow* (**249**) which represents the culmination of the Byzantine style in Russia and shows also how far Russian Byzantine forms had diverged from Constantinople and the West.

Kiev

Byzantine architecture was introduced to three principal centres in Russia: *Kiev, Novgorod* and *Vladimir*. The earliest of these was at Kiev where, in 988, Vladimir, Grand Duke of Kiev was converted to Christianity and from this time onwards he and his successors encouraged commerce and cultural exchange between the area and Constantinople. Architects and craftsmen came to Russia to build the first churches and to share their experience with the Russians. At that time Kiev was one of Russia's greatest cities and within half a century had a great cathedral and hundreds of churches. However, in 1239 the city succumbed to Tartar invasion and much of the Byzantine architecture was destroyed while church building developed further in areas which suffered less from barbarian attacks. It was the ambition of Vladimir and his son Yaroslav to create at Kiev a city as fine as Constantinople and they planned monasteries, churches and schools. Early buildings were in wood and have perished, but parts of later stone ones survive.

Cathedral of S. Sophia, begun 1037

This building was the first great Byzantine church in Russia and it set the pattern for innumerable smaller churches. It is difficult to define accurately what it was like for, although it still exists, it has been damaged, altered and restored so the original design has been obscured. Only in recent years, due to patient work, is its early form beginning to be discernible. It is a brick, cross-domed basilica, its plan clearly based on Constantinople pattern, and was originally nearly square in plan, with a central dome about 25 feet in diameter and 12 smaller domes (to represent Christ and his apostles). It had aisles and five semi-circular apses (**237**). Later, four more aisles were added, each terminating in a round apse, thus giving an east end with nine apses (**238**). It also gained two western towers and eight more domes. After the sack of the city in 1239 the cathedral fell into decay until the seventeenth century, but even in this ruinous state greatly impressed travellers of the period. In the eighteenth century it was restored and the domes added (**239**). Although based on Byzantine type plan, S. Sophia, even in the eleventh century, had acquired individual Russian characteristics. This was evidenced in the 13 domes and their arrangement. They were low domes set on tall, narrow drums, possibly based in design upon the wooden Cathedral of S. Sophia at Novgorod (destroyed by fire 1045). The church was also surrounded on three sides (except the east) by an open arcade on which a gallery was later built. Inside, the piers were massive and there were more of them than in examples further west. Also the interior was higher and narrower, both characteristics being necessary to support the 13 domes. Unfortunately, as elsewhere in the tenth and eleventh centuries, the Russians followed Byzantine building methods closely in, for example, laying the tiled roofs directly upon the vaults. This was suitable in a Mediterranean climate but fatal in Russia. The Russians learnt to adapt this system to their climate as they adapted roof and dome pitches for the same reason.

Today, the exterior of S. Sophia is very much like the eighteenth century model in the cathedral (**239**). The lower part is of the simpler Medieval Byzantine period while the domes and drums are more Baroque. The building is surrounded by walls and the visitor enters through the great bell tower gateway. Inside the cathedral there is more light than is usual in such great Byzantine churches. This is because there are so many domes and the lantern of each is pierced with windows. In addition there is a large western lunette window. An unfortunate ornate gilt altar screen obscures the simplicity of the vertical lines of the great eastern apse, but above is visible the mosaic in the conch depicting the Virgin against a gilt background; below are saints and apostles. In the crossing cupola are mosaics of the Christ Pantocrator with four angels around him. The great piers dividing nave and aisles and the smaller octagonal columns are fresco covered.

Not only did *Byzantine churches* in *Kiev* suffer from barbarian invasion in the Middle Ages, but damage to these fabrics in the Second World War was devastating. On the fringe of the city, now in the Botanic Garden of the Academy, still stands the *Monastery of Vydubitsky* which contains the churches of *S. Michael* and *S. George*. The latter dates from the eighteenth century but S. Michael was built in the eleventh century and much of it survives. Of the famous *Lavra Monastery* on the ridge of hills overlooking the Dnieper river on the outskirts of Kiev little exists from Medieval building. One enters by the gateway underneath the *Church of the Trinity 'on the Porch'*. This was a combined church and look-out gateway and was constructed early in the twelfth century. The interior, consisting of two lookout rooms on the ground floor, has been well preserved, and the church above with central cupola supported on four piers. The exterior was decorated in the eighteenth century with Baroque frescoes (**865**). The masterpiece of the monastery was the centrally placed *Cathedral of the Assumption*, built in the late twelfth century and, due to its fine proportions and construction, used many times as a model to later churches. It had been redecorated in Baroque style in the eighteenth century, but its Medieval character had been retained until it was wantonly destroyed by order of the Germans in the Second World War. The remainder of the Lavra buildings are of eighteenth and nineteenth century construction.

At *Chernigov*, a few miles north-east of Kiev, is the *Cathedral of the Transfiguration*, begun 1031 and the *Church of S. Paraskeva*, 1118. These two examples are of similar design; they are cross-domed basilicas with short western arms and apsidal east ends. The cathedral has five domes on drums, the central one supported on four piers. The building was richly decorated in marble and fresco but little of this remains.

Novgorod and Pskov

Novgorod (new town) was, despite its name, an old settlement which, by the tenth century, had become an important trade centre. It had regular contacts with Constantinople, notwithstanding its northern position (near the city of Leningrad), by means of the river Dnieper and the Black Sea. More important still, it was the only large town in Russia not ravaged by barbarian invasion in the thirteenth century, due to its marshy situation on the shores of Lake Ilmen, so it was able to expand and become wealthy. It was an artistic and cultural centre as well as a commercial one and retained its importance until the rise of Moscow in the fifteenth century. Its tenth century architecture was strongly influenced by that of Kiev. For nearly 500 years the people of this area built churches, cathedrals, schools and houses on the Byzantine model and, as time passed, adapted these designs to their own needs. Thus, while Kiev was the originator in Russia of Byzantine architecture, Novgorod was the district where this architecture became Russianised and indigenous. Building was primarily in wood, because of the quantity of timber in the area, but was also in brick and stone. The complex Kiev church plans were soon adapted to simpler

THE CATHEDRAL OF S. SOPHIA, KIEV, U.S.S.R.

237 The Cathedral as it existed in the thirteenth
century. Drawn from a model now in the cathedral

238 Plan. Of the same date

239 Cathedral as it was redesigned in the eighteenth
century and as it has been restored now. Model of
eighteenth century version also in Cathedral

versions of four piers supporting one dome and with three apses at the east end of the church. Wall surfaces were covered with stucco and then painted white. Cornices and drums were decorated in brick with zig-zag and saw-tooth ornament. The climate of this region was largely responsible for the adaptation of Byzantine roofing methods. Low pitched Byzantine roofs and hemispherical domes were unsuitable for snow and rain so the people of Novgorod developed roofs of steeper pitch with onion domes. It is disputed whether these onion domes were a development indigenous to the area or whether the idea came from further east, but the former seems more likely on the weight of evidence; they were being built by the mid-twelfth century here and were designed in a great variety of shapes and in large numbers.

Cathedral of S. Sophia

The first cathedral of this name in Novgorod was built in wood soon after Vladimir's conversion to Christianity in 988. It typified the northern Russian timber interpretation of Byzantine architecture just as the cathedral at Kiev illustrated that of southern Russia in masonry. It was destroyed by fire in 1045 and a new cathedral was begun soon after. This time the building was in stone and was a simpler edition of its namesake in Kiev. It is smaller and has five aisles and three eastern apses. There are six lofty, tapering, bulbous domes on tall cylindrical drums. Inside, the great piers curve up the interior space and emphasise the verticality of the design. The twelfth century frescoes have now been restored.

There are a number of *churches* still surviving in the area. The twelfth century examples are simple and tall with nave, single aisles, three apses carried the full height of the building and a tall cupola covering the crossing supported on six piers. Some churches have further domes over the west end. The exterior form is tall, cubical and very simple and represents the beginning of a national style. Extant examples include the *Nativity of the Virgin*, 1117, in the Monastery of S. Anthony, *S. George*, 1119–30, in the Yuriev (George) Monastery and *S. Nicholas*, 1113. In the thirteenth and fourteenth centuries designs were further simplified and nationalised. Piers were reduced from six to four, the apse became shallower and often single, the aisles were

decreased in height and width. Many churches had four simple gables of equal size one on each face, surmounted by a central dome upon a drum. Examples of this style include the *Church of S. Theodore Stratilates*, 1360–2 and the *Transfiguration*, 1374, both in the commercial quarter of Novgorod. Later churches are represented by *S. Peter* and *S. Paul*, 1406, and the *Twelve Apostles*, 1450. Near to the town is also the *Church of the Annunciation*, 1179, at Lake Miatchine. One of the finest churches was that dedicated to the *Saviour at Nereditski*, 1198, which was completely destroyed in the Second World War.

Pskov, a town north-west from Novgorod, also established independent architectural expression, in similar form, in the Middle Ages, but the work was simpler and cruder. The city remained free until the early sixteenth century but was less wealthy. A basic difference in the architectural construction was the use in Pskov of corbelled arches rather than pendentives to support the domes. This was partly due to economy and partly to inexperience. Examples of churches remaining include *S. Sergius, S. Cosmos* and *S. Damian*, all of the fourteenth century.

Vladimir

After the decline of Kiev, a new centre of power and influence was slowly established in the region of Moscow. Craftsmen had fled from Kiev and brought their architecture with them. Two such centres were *Vladimir* and *Suzdal*. The architectural style of the region was derived partly from Kiev but was also influenced by Novgorod and by Western Byzantine culture. Later in the twelfth century Vladimir became the capital and leading city of the area and continued so until it succumbed to the Tartars. Much of the finest building dates from the twelfth century. Churches were built of white sandstone, in contrast to brick at Kiev and wood at Novgorod, and followed a simple plan with one bulbous dome over the crossing supported on four piers and three round, high apses at the east end.

The *Cathedral of the Assumption* (Dormition), now called the Uspensky Cathedral, was built in 1158 but rebuilt after a fire in 1183. It was based upon the designs of S. Sophia in Kiev and is, therefore, more elaborate in plan than is usual in

240

240 *Cathedral of the Assumption, Vladimir, U.S.S.R., twelfth century*

this region. It is a double-aisled church and has a central dome and four more over the angles. The central dome is supported on pendentives and the smaller ones on squinches (240). The interior was richly decorated with fresco paintings but much of this has been lost. The *Cathedral of S. Dimitri* was begun in 1194 and has a simpler plan with four piers supporting a single dome. It is a large, solidly built church and particularly finely decorated on the exterior by carved decoration on the upper walls and drums, also on the portals (one on each side) and corbel tables. It is a mixture of Romanesque and Byzantine designs, both in Russian style. The lower parts of the walls were restored in the eighteenth century and represent biblical scenes.

Outside the city, nearby, are some further examples. The *Church of SS. Boris* and *Gleb* was built in 1152 on the bank of the river Nerl near Suzdal in the village of *Kideksha*. Much of

the exterior, however, has beem damaged. At *Pereyaslavl-Zalesski* is the *Cathedral of the Transfiguration*, 1158, built in white stone, which is in better condition. It has a single dome (rebuilt in the sixteenth century) supported on four piers and a tri-apsidal east end. The roof rests directly on the church vaults. The *Church of the Protection and Intercession of the Virgin*, 1165 (the Church of Pokrov) is also near the river Nerl where it joins the river Klyazma. It is a well-preserved and particularly fine example and one of the four early churches extant. It has the single dome on four piers and three eastern apses. The walls are thick, pierced by splayed window and door openings. There is some of the earliest surviving Russian sculpture here; on the upper section of the three façades are carved relief figures and carved corbel blocks. These, together with the west doorway decoration, display a Romanesque quality.

MONASTERIES AND CATHEDRALS IN MOSCOW

241 Cathedral of the Annunciation in the Kremlin, 1482–9, Pskov architects

242 View and 243 plan of the Smolenski Monastery Cathedral, c. 1525, bell-tower seventeenth century, Moscow

244 Cathedral of the Assumption (Dormition) in the Kremlin, 1475–9, Aristotele Fioravanti

CHURCHES AND MONASTERIES IN AND NEAR MOSCOW

245 Corner octagonal tower of the Church of the Decapitation of S. John the Baptist, Dyakovo, near Moscow, sixteenth century

246 Church of the Nativity of the Virgin in Putinki, Moscow, c. 1650

247 Monastery of the Virgin of the Don, near Moscow, 1593

248 Andronikhov Monastery. Church of the Saviour, Moscow, 1425

Moscow

Until the fall of Constantinople in 1453 Russian Christian architecture had been directly inspired and assisted by artists and craftsmen from the Empire. In the late fifteenth century the new centre of power and culture in a unified Russia was being established in *Moscow*. The residence of the Metropolitan had been transferred here from Vladimir and Ivan III (the Great), 1462–1505, had the wooden buildings of the Kremlin largely rebuilt in more durable materials. After 150 years of Tartar domination Russia was recovering and, since the fall of Constantinople, architects and craftsmen came to Moscow to advise and build Ivan's now permanent city. In Western Europe this was the beginning of the Renaissance and the change from Medievalism to classicism; in Russia also there was a new era but not a Renaissance. It was an entirely new architectural age and one commonly called *Muscovite* since much of its force and inspiration came from the Princes of Moscow. The new *Moscow churches* still followed the Byzantine ground plan and inside were decorated with Byzantine style mosaic and fresco on walls with few interrupting mouldings, but outside Renaissance ornament made its appearance, introduced by the Italian craftsmen who brought their new style with them. Often, instead of a central dome, a tall steeple would be built; this was no Gothic spire, but a traditional Russian design in pyramidal form. Gradually, by weaving together all these different influences and ideas, a truly Russian architectural form was evolved which, by the sixteenth century, was entirely national and its chief example is the *Cathedral of S. Basil*.

The Cathedrals of the Kremlin

When Ivan III came to the throne the Kremlin hill was still covered with wooden buildings. The reconstruction he undertook was largely completed in his own reign. Much of this work was comprised in the cathedrals of the Kremlin. The first of these was the new *Cathedral of the Assumption* (Dormition), 1475–9, which was the primary church of Russia and the seat of the Metropolitan of Moscow (**244**). The cathedral was begun by Russian architects in 1471 but part of the building collapsed in the earthquake of 1472 so the work was handed over to an Italian architect and engineer, *Aristotele Fioravanti* from *Bologna*. His terms of reference were to design a building based on the Cathedral of the Dormition in Vladimir and which would be structurally sound. He carried out this commission and built a five-domed cathedral in cubical mass. It is, however, an unusual building in that, although it conforms to the Vladimir plan and Byzantine pattern, the architect introduced Italian fifteenth century building methods, using light bricks and tie rods in the arches and vaults. By his skill in design and execution he blended the Italian Renaissance with Russian Byzantine so that in decoration, particularly on the exterior, the roofing and lighting, the whole effect is more modern and classical than the Vladimir prototype. The Assumption in Moscow became the new prototype and was copied again and again all over Russia for many years as the orthodox pattern for such great churches.

The second *Cathedral* is that of the *Annunciation*, built 1482–90 by architects from Pskov (**241**). Here also the model was the Vladimir Cathedral but this design is much more in the tradition of Russian Byzantine architecture. It was built with five domes and three eastern apses and has entrances on three sides. In the sixteenth century further galleries and chapels were added.

In and near Moscow are a number of other monasteries and churches built between the fifteenth and seventeenth centuries, all of Byzantine character but displaying individually Russian features particularly in the domes and the stepped ogee, triangular and rounded shell formations (called *kokoshniki*)* which topped the main building and acted as a base for the tower or cupola drums. Such examples include the early *Church of the Saviour* (1425) in the *Andronikhov Monastery* in the city (**248**) and the *Monastery of the Virgin of the Don* (1593) which is on the outskirts (**247**). A most colourful version is a small but richly decorative church in the centre of Moscow, the *Church of the Nativity of the Virgin in Putinki* (c. 1650) which is now closed to the public. It is surrounded by modern blocks, but nevertheless well preserved on the exterior (**246**).

On one of the hills but still in the city, is the *Smolenski Monastery*, built in 1524–5 as a memorial for the victory and return of the city of Smolensk to Russia (**242** and **243**). This is one

A kokoshnik is a traditional, feminine head-dress. The arches were thought to resemble this.

249

249 The Cathedral of S. Basil the Blessed, Red Square, Moscow, 1554–1679, Postnik and Barma

of the most ancient buildings in Moscow and a very early stone structure. The cathedral here bears considerable resemblance to the Assumption Cathedral in the Kremlin. Under it is constructed a sixteenth century mausoleum and behind (**242**) is the seventeenth century bell tower. The interior walls are entirely fresco covered. The five tall domes are supported on steeply sloping pendentives.

A few miles outside Moscow on a ridge of hills sloping steeply down to the river Moskva below is the *Church of the Decapitation of S. John the Baptist* at *Dyakovo* (**245**), which is only about a mile away across the trees and woods from the unusual *Church of the Ascension* at *Kolomenskoe* (Chapter 5, Fig. **560**). S. John's Church is octagonal, with plain ribbed walls and four openings. One of these is the main doorway, one leads to the apsidal altar chamber and the others to side entrances. It is an immensely tall church, ascending to a diminishing lantern form with windows and with a tall steeple above. This main octagon is the central chamber or nave. At four corners are smaller octagons, replicas in design of the large one and all very tall. One of these is shown in Fig. **245**. An ambulatory round the central octagon joins together the four chapels of the smaller ones.

A fitting finale to Russian architecture based on Byzantine form is the great *Cathedral Church of S. Basil the Blessed* (Vasili Blazheni) in the Red Square of *Moscow*. Begun by Ivan the Terrible in 1554, designed by two Russian architects *Postnik* and *Barma*, it was not completed until 1679. It is different from any Byzantine architecture in east or west but owes much of its fundamental character to the Byzantine style. It represents the logical conclusion to preceding buildings and is the expression of national culture; it stands for the essence of Muscovite Christianity in Russia and was the last great church of the movement in this architectural form. In plan it is simple and almost symmetrical but three-dimensionally it is complex: a bizarre, richly coloured building. The central part of the cathedral stands, like the Ascension Church at Kolomenskoe, on a high platform and has a tall octagonal tower. On the four main axes are set four large octagonal chapels, each with towers, while at the angles between these are four smaller polygonal chapels. These are all surmounted by bulbous domes, and in the seventeenth century the brilliant polychrome decorative colour was completed, giving the cathedral its characteristic Russian appearance (**249**).

4
Civic Planning and the Grid Town Layout

GREEK TOWN PLANNING

The idea of designing the layout of a town for aesthetic and practical considerations, of providing order and convenience for the social and defensive needs of its citizens, is an old one. The grid scheme of city layout with streets crossing one another at right angles and with a uniformity of street width and building design, which became the pattern for the classical world of Greece and Rome and was later adopted in Europe and modern America, was developed in Ionian Greece from the seventh century B.C.; this street pattern is often referred to as *Milesian* because it is named after the city of *Miletos* on the coast of Asia Minor.

The grid street plan is believed to have originated earlier and further east, possibly in Mesopotamia, but the concept is familiarly associated with the name of *Hippodamos*, a Greek philosopher and town planner who lived in the early fifth century B.C. This is due to Aristotle who ascribed its invention to Hippodamos who was born in Miletos. In the reconstruction of the city about 475 B.C., after its sack by the Persians, Hippodamos was able to put forward his ideas on urban planning. These included the concept of dividing up a city into three areas, one for public buildings, one for sacred use and the third for private homes. In Miletos, for instance, the central area was reserved for the *agora*, which was an open-air meeting place for the transaction of business, comprising a market place, stoas and commercial halls. (A stoa was a long, colonnaded building which contained shops and offices and enabled people to shop or carry out their business in privacy and protected from rain or hot sun). Residential areas surrounded the agora and excavation has revealed parts of the grid pattern here, containing some hundreds of uniform rectangular blocks.

It is not certain whether Hippodamos was ever in charge of laying out a town but his plans and ideas were influential in the planning of some cities, for example, Piraeus, the port of Athens, in about 470–460 B.C.

Tholoi

Often this type of structure, utilised for various purposes, was part of the plan in the city *agora*. A simple design of diameter some 65 feet, was part of the administrative centre in the *agora* in Athens. It was constructed *c.* 470 B.C. and was used as a meeting place. The plain exterior circular walls partly supported the covering conical roof but, inside, six columns set on elliptical plan, assisted in this support. (**I**).

Hellenistic Towns

The Hellenistic age dates from the time of the victories of Alexander the Great (PLATE 39). His conquest of the Persian Empire, completed in 330 B.C., brought a new prosperity to the cities of Asia Minor. Some of these were enlarged, others rebuilt on fresh sites. Alexander's campaigns resulted in a blending of the purer Greek form of art and architecture with the ideas on construction, function and ornament which stemmed from a Greek Empire greatly extended towards, and influenced from, the east. In architecture there appeared a greater variety of buildings for different purposes. The character and proportions of the orders changed: columns were slenderer, taller and spaced further apart and entablatures became narrower. There was a marked increase in rich decoration. The Corinthian Order was now used. The Greeks remained cautious in their use of the arch and vault but, by the second century B.C., both semi-circular and segmental arches were being more widely employed.

Town planning especially in the Hellenistic cities of Asia Minor had become more important. The grid pattern of streets was extensively adopted and the areas for religious, civic and private building carefully laid out. *Priene* was rebuilt near the mouth of the River Meander about 334 B.C. Because the town was not of great importance under the late Roman rule, few alterations were made to adapt it to Roman needs, so much of the Hellenistic building has survived. Priene was built on Milesian plan; it is probably the best and one of the oldest of such grid plans amongst Hellenistic cities. *Pergamon* was an imposing hillside city and full advantage was taken of this dramatic site. Approached from the sea the effect was magnificent as the buildings extended from the lower Sanctuary of Asklepios to the middle city with its gymnasia, its agora and sacred precinct to the upper acropolis city with its important temples, steeply sloping theatre cut into the hillside and famous Altar of Zeus.

In a Hellenistic town the *agora* had now acquired a greater importance; large cities such as Ephesos and Pergamon possessed more than one. The commercial agora on Ephesos was one of the largest and most impressive in the world. Usually the agora was bounded on three sides by *stoas* which had now become more elaborate in design. Many were two-storeyed and followed a custom not familar in the classical period of Greece in that two orders appeared on the front colonnade, Doric

on the ground floor and Ionic above as in the rebuilt *Stoa of Attalos II of Pergamon* in the *agora of Athens* (**38**). A wide stoa now needed an internal colonnade to support the roof; this was usually in the Ionic Order with tall column shafts. The stoa at Priene is an example of this. Behind this colonnade shops and offices were built against the rear wall.

In the agora was also to be found the administrative council house—the *bouleuterion* or senate house—of which interesting remains survive especially at *Priene, Termessos* and *Miletos*. The last of these was the most elaborate. Erected 175–164 B.C. by Timarchos and Heraklides, it comprised a propylon, a colonnaded courtyard and an auditorium. The Corinithian Order was used for the propylon which had three entrances. Three sides of the courtyard were colonnaded in the Doric Order. On the fourth side was the meeting chamber or auditorium which provided seating for over 1200 persons. Its wooden roof was supported by the walls and four Ionic columns (**II**).

Among other important structures were *libraries, gymnasia* and *public baths*. These baths, like the early Roman ones at Pompeii, included dressing rooms and latrines, as well as chambers provided with different air and water temperatures.

Temples in Asia Minor

Surviving remains date chiefly from the Hellenistic period; in consequence, the columns are taller and slenderer than in earlier times and have a wider intercolumniation. These proportional changes

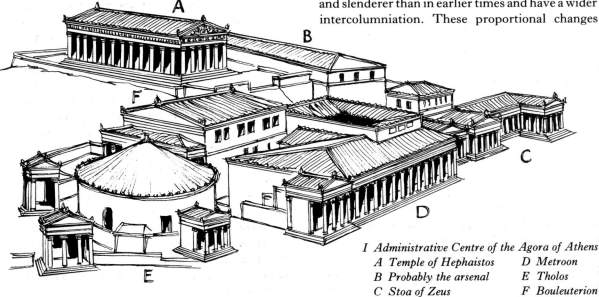

I *Administrative Centre of the Agora of Athens*
A *Temple of Hephaistos*   D *Metroon*
B *Probably the arsenal*   E *Tholos*
C *Stoa of Zeus*   F *Bouleuterion*

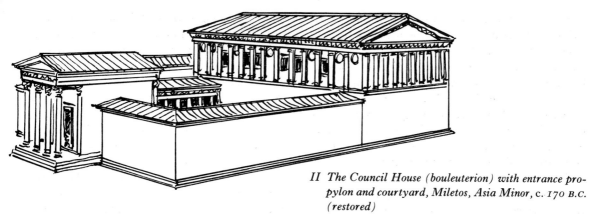

II *The Council House (bouleuterion) with entrance propylon and courtyard, Miletos, Asia Minor, c. 170 B.C. (restored)*

rendered the design of the Greek Doric Order, with its baseless thick and shorter columns, more difficult and temples built here from about 300 B.C. onwards were most commonly of the Ionic Order or, occasionally Corinthian Order construction. The most notable examples were built at *Didyma*, *Ephesos*, *Priene* and *Sardis*. They were very large evidencing the importance of the cities being replanned and reconstructed at this time.

The building of the Hellenistic *Temple of Apollo* at *Didyma* was begun in the late fourth century B.C. and work continued into the early years of the Roman Empire. It was not the first temple on the site. The first archaic temple was begun in the late eighth century B.C. and, between 560 and 550 B.C., the great archaic temple was fully completed. Didyma was a coastal port near to the important city of Miletos (page 143), connected to it by the sacred road. After Alexander the Great had regained independence for the Ionian cities he initiated the building of a new and large temple, dedicated to Apollo, on the site of the earlier building. This Hellenistic temple was the third largest structure of its time. Designed by the architects Paionios of Ephesos and Daphnis of Miletos, this dipteral decastyle temple measured 356 feet by 168 feet in plan, its 120 Ionic columns rising to 65 feet in height. A considerable portion of the temple still stands and, even in its ruined condition, presents a most impressive sight. Particularly imposing is the variety of column bases dating from Hellenistic and Roman times and the sculptural fragments such as the Medusa head from the temple frieze (PLATE 36).

The *Temple of Artemis* at *Ephesos* was even larger than the Didyma temple and measured 391 feet by 211 feet in plan. Erected by the Ephesians in 334–250 B.C., on the site of an earlier temple which, partly constructed of wood, had been burnt down in 356 B.C., the new temple—one of the seven wonders of the ancient world—was the finest great structure in the Greek world to be built of marble, as well as being, to date, the largest temple constructed. Its architects were Paionios and Demetrios. The building was famous for the quality and quantity of its sculpture and notable artists such as Scopas contributed to the temple decoration. Any projected reconstruction of this great temple has been made very difficult by the fragmentation and scattering of the remains but in recent years Anton Bammer has published the results of his work on the site in *Die Architektur des Jüngeren Artemision von Ephesos*, Wiesbaden, 1972.

Five complete columns remain standing of the *Temple of Athena* built on the highest part of the city of *Priene*. The temple, the oldest (340–250 B.C.) and most important building of the city, was the work of Pytheos, architect of the Mausoleum of Halicarnassos (page 35) and, though of more modest dimensions (122 feet by 64 feet), than the temples at Didyma and Ephesos, was finely proportioned and regarded as a model for Ionic temples in Asia Minor. The architect published a book explaining his work here and his principles of architectural design.

The large Ionic *Temple of Artemis* at *Sardis* seems to have been built in three phases. Begun about 300 B.C., work was continued between 175–150 B.C. and a further construction period in Roman times resulted in various alterations about A.D. 150. A number of columns, capitals and bases survive from the different buildings periods, including the Ionic capital (PLATE 5) dating from the 300 B.C. work.

Plate 36 Head of Medusa from the frieze of the Temple of Apollo, Didyma, Turkey, second century A.D.

Plate 37 Base of a monument to Diocletian, Rome

Greek Domestic Architecture

A quantity of remains of domestic building survives in, particularly *Priene* in Asia Minor, the *Island of Delos* in Greece and *Pompeii* in Italy. In Priene some houses survive in part from the fourth to the second century B.C., in Delos and Pompeii the structures date mainly from the second century B.C. Houses were inward-looking, few window and door openings breaking the blank exterior walls. Inside were one- or two-storeyed colonnaded courts. Stone or marble was used for the lower parts of the walls, the upper being of sun-dried brick and timber. Many houses consisted of one storey only but in a number of instances, as at Priene, stairs have been excavated, leading to the presumption that an upper story had been constructed. Floors were mosaic- or tile-covered,

walls painted. There were living rooms, bedrooms, bathrooms and latrines. Each house contained a place for worship with an altar (**III**, **IV**).

On the Island of Delos some of the later houses, built *c.* 150–50 B.C., extended upwards for up to four storeys; they have survived extremely well (**III**). The problems of providing adequate water supplies for a large population on an island with no running water were considerable so bathrooms were less common, though latrines were built. The roofs of houses drained into the internal courts, the water being collected in a cistern beneath. Rain falling on to the theatre nearby was collected in a channel circling the orchestra to fill a large rock-cut storage cistern. This was vaulted over and the construction arches of the vault survive remarkably intact (PLATE 38).

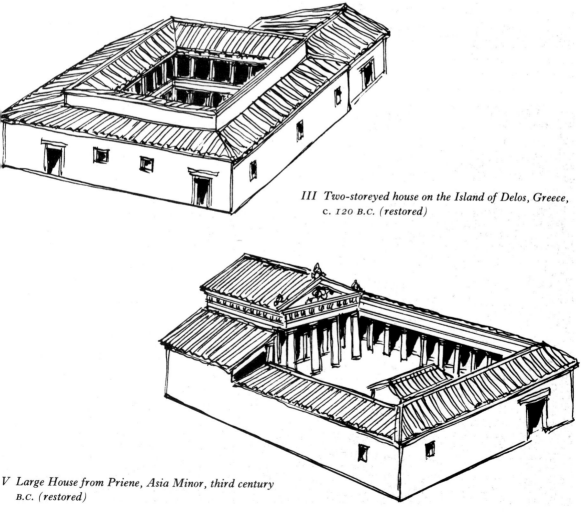

III Two-storeyed house on the Island of Delos, Greece, c. 120 B.C. (restored)

V Large House from Priene, Asia Minor, third century B.C. (restored)

Plate 38
Cistern, Island of Delos

ETRUSCAN BUILDING

The cultural history of ancient Italy differed from that of the Aegean area. Before the coming of the Etruscans there was no advanced form of art and architecture. From the later seventh century B.C. the Greeks colonized Sicily and southern Italy but it was the Etruscans who introduced a high culture to the central area of the peninsular.

The Etruscans (named Etrusci or Tusci in Greek or Latin) called themselves the Rasenna. It is believed that they migrated to central Italy from Asia Minor or possibly further east in the eighth century B.C.; remaining dominant and independent until the third century B.C. after which they were gradually Latinised under Roman rule.

The Etruscans lived an urban life in fine cities and were capable of a high standard in building and the visual and literary arts. Over five centuries they developed their own art and architecture, which were derived from Greek and oriental sources, but adapted to their needs in Italy. Greek influence was particularly strong upon their culture. Remains are not extensive and no complete buildings survive intact; there are, though, many examples of walling, gateways, arches and tombs (**68–84**).

They were great builders and masons. In their stone walling they used large blocks, often polygonal, without cement. Later they constructed arches with radiating voussoirs—though they were not the inventors in Europe of this type of construction: the Greeks were building in this way from the fifth century. In their tombs the Etruscans skilfully constructed high vaults of dressed stone, some corbelled out, pointing the way towards the later, pendentive method of covering a square-wall building with a circular-based domed covering

(**V**). By the sixth century they had mastered advanced timber construction. They used sun-dried bricks widely, their bricks being of Lydian proportion, thin and measuring about 12 × 18 inches. Like the Minoans, they often combined brick bases with an upper structure of timber.

Early Etruscan towns were built on hills, surrounded by low walls. By the fifth century, higher, fortress-walling with city gates was being constructed to protect the towns from Roman attack. The Etruscans introduced the Greek grid town plan to Italy. Though little domestic building survives, much has been learnt of its style from the tomb interiors decorated by painting, terracotta and metal.

The temple was important in Etruscan life and temples were built in the centre of towns. Foundation remains show the ground plan but reconstruction of the superstructure has to be more speculative. There appears to have been a colonnaded pronaos in front with a wide intercolumniation. The entablature and columns were usually of wood. Temple design differed from the Greek pattern in that the building was erected on a podium with front approach steps. The temple also was colonnaded. Ornamentation was by rich terracotta work (**76** and **VI**).

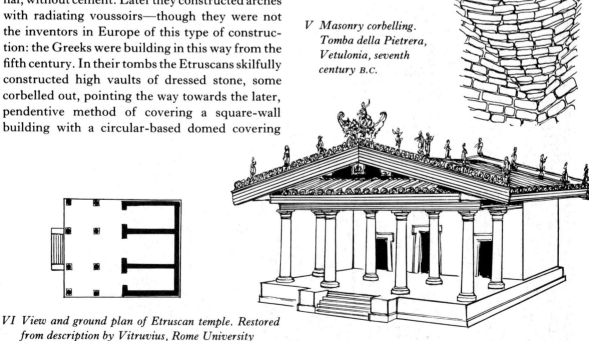

V Masonry corbelling. Tomba della Pietrera, Vetulonia, seventh century B.C.

VI View and ground plan of Etruscan temple. Restored from description by Vitruvius, Rome University

Versions of the Doric and Ionic Order were used, the columns sometimes fluted. The Doric capitals were large and simple, the Ionic ones of the Aeolic type. Vitruvius also refers to a variation on the Doric Order which he calls Tuscan; this has an unfluted column shaft which stands upon an Ionic-type base (**VII** and **VIII**).

VII Doric column. Tomb at Cerveteri, sixth century B.C.
VIII Tuscan pillar, Cerveteri, third century B.C.

ANCIENT ROME

Building Construction

Concrete had long been utilized as a bonding and covering material but it was the Romans who developed it as a structural one. By the second century B.C. they were experimenting with a volcanic earth found near Vesuvius and named pozzolana after the town of Pozzuoli there. Pozzolana is a volcanic ash, available in quantity in Italy, containing alumina and silica, which combines chemically with lime to produce a hard, durable substance. The Romans mixed it with an aggregate of broken stone, marble, brick and lava, and poured it over wood centering and into brick compartments. This method of construction is illustrated in Figs. **IX** and **X**. Similar types of kiln-burnt bricks were utilised to make the piers for the Roman system of hypocaust under-floor heating (page 63 and **XI**).

IX Building a brick and concrete arch over wood centering
    A Brick voussoirs
    B Wood centering
    C Springing line of arch
X Building a brick and concrete vault
    A Wood centering
    B Brick structure
    C Concrete infilling

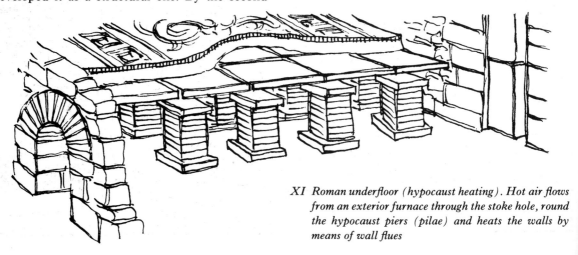

XI Roman underfloor (hypocaust heating). Hot air flows from an exterior furnace through the stoke hole, round the hypocaust piers (pilae) and heats the walls by means of wall flues

The use of concrete and brick was adopted on a grand scale to make possible the construction of massive piers supporting vault spans of a magnitude unequalled until the steel structures of modern times (page 49). Such interiors as the great basilicas and even larger halls of the public bathing establishments illustrated such building techniques on the greatest scale (pages 55–7, 63, 65–6 and **XII** and **XIII**).

Temples in Asia Minor
Here the Hellenistic tradition of temple building continued well into Imperial Roman times. Many temples had survived constructed of permanent materials, and these provided a pattern to follow. Only slowly was the Roman temple form adopted of an entrance façade and a podium base. Temples in the area were large, the Ionic Order predominating. Remains are not extensive. Notable is the *Temple of Trajan* at *Pergamon*, completed *c.* A.D. 130, which stands on the summit of the acropolis city. It is of hexastyle peripteral design. In *Ephesos*

is the modest-sized *Temple of Hadrian* which displays the Mesopotamian tradition of an arched lintel, a device introduced from Syria in the first century (**133**). Much larger was the *Temple of Serapis* here but now only in fragments after earthquake destruction. A number of columns remain erect of the Ionic *Temple of Aphrodite* at *Aphrodisias*, a structure which was adapted into a Christian basilica in the fifth century A.D.

Baths in Asia Minor
The structure and layout here of the great bathing establishments were not carbon copies of those in Italy; many were more extensive and elaborate and their design was affected by the existence on most sites of the Hellenistic gymnasium which, in itself, had become a sophisticated layout, providing not only facilities for gymnastic exercise, but also social, artistic and educational activities. This overlapped to a considerable degree the Roman bath concept and adaptations had to be made in the Imperial Roman period.

XII Reconstructed interior of the Basilica of Maxentius (Constantine) c. A.D. 307–20

XIII Reconstruction of the great hall of the Baths of Caracalla, Rome, c. A.D. 212–16

Extensive bathing establishments were constructed under the Empire in all cities and substantial remains exist in, especially, Ephesos, Miletos, Pergamon, Hierapolis and Aphrodisias. At *Ephesos*, as in Rome, baths were constructed in various parts of the city, notably those built at the *Vedius gymnasium*, (mid-second century A.D.), the immense complex down at the *harbour* (second century A.D) and the smaller *Scholastikia Baths*, enlarged in the fourth century A.D. and situated on the marble sacred street. Most impressive also were the East and West Baths at the *Upper Gymnasium* at *Pergamon* (first and second centuries A.D.), the *Faustina Baths* at *Miletos* (161–80 A.D.), those built over the mineral springs at *Hierapolis* (second century A.D.) and the *Hadrian Baths* at *Aphrodisias*.

Theatres in Asia Minor

Here are the most ambitious theatres, and those with the most impressive remains. Every town of importance possessed its theatre most of which had been built in Hellenistic times often carved out of the hillside but fronted by a stage building and proscenium platform. In Imperial Roman times many of these theatres were altered. In some cases the orchestra area was reduced from a horseshoe form to a semicircular one, seating space was enlarged and access provided by vaulted passageways. Characteristic are those at *Miletos*, a large theatre seating over 15,000 spectators, *Ephesos* with a seating capacity of 24,000 and *Perge* which retains some of its marble thrones and parts of its richly sculptured scene building. The superbly sited Hellenistic theatres at the citadel of *Pergamon* and *Termessos* were only slightly altered in Roman times. Both are carved deeply out of the mountainside and their steeply sloping auditoria seating gives a superb view of the plains below.

The theatres at *Side* and *Aspendos* were built on Roman lines in the second century A.D. At Side the theatre is supported on barrel-vaulted sub-structures. Its exterior façade was a two-storey arcade (the lower one well-preserved) with superimposed orders. The magnificent theatre at Aspendos is the best preserved example of antiquity. Here is a Roman theatre built over barrel-vaulted substructures but gently resting in part against the hillside. As at Side, though, the horseshoe orchestra form has been preserved. The Aspendos stage building is particularly complete both on the auditorium side and the exterior façade (**XIV**).

XIV The Theatre at Aspendos, Asia Minor, A.D. 161–80. A rare example in the preservation of the stage building comprising the two-storeyed façade and the proscenium upon which the play was performed

Domestic Building

Throughout the Roman Empire this was of three main types: the *domus* (town house), the *inula* (apartment block) and the *villa* (country house). The layout and design of the domus was derived from its Hellenistic prototype as built on Delos and at Priene (page 82),. It was designed for middle class and well-to-do families. It had a narrow street façade, its entrance flanked by shops. The rectangular site extended well back from the street. The house was planned to be inwardly orientated towards open colonnaded courtyards where rainwater was collected from the sloping roofs of the *compluvium* (open central square) to the *impluvium* (a receptacle below). Rooms were arranged round the atrium and colonnaded garden courts (peristyles) so shades or sun could be enjoyed at all seasons and time of day.

With a rapidly increasing urbanization of a growing population, the majority of city-dwellers lived in flats. Such a flat (cenaculum) would be in an apartment block (insula). In Pompeii such blocks were generally of two storeys, constructed of brick and timber. Later *insulae*, considerable remains of which may be seen at Ostia, were built of concrete and brick and could rise to four or five storeys. In the city of Rome it is believed that some

40,000 *insulae* lined the streets and squares. Life in a *cenaculum* was overcrowded and lacked many basic amenities, hence the popularity of the bathing establishments.

The rural *villa* was a larger, spreading layout. It was a self-sufficient unit comprising farm buildings and accommodation for slaves, servants, artisans and family. It would include buildings and areas for baking, storage, wine- and textile-making as well as all farming needs (**XV**).

Civic design

In Asia Minor *Ephesos* was the most important centre. In Roman times it became the capital city of the province of Asia and the principal port for all of south-west Anatolia. Apart from the theatre, temples and baths already discussed (pages 82, 83), excavation has disclosed extensive and impressive remains. In addition to the Upper Agora (the state agora) there was a commercial (Lower) *agora*. Built in Hellenistic times this market place was greatly enlarged in the first and second centuries A.D. to become one of the largest in the Roman world. It was of square plan, each side measuring over 350 feet and completely enclosed by stoas. Nearby was the important *Celsus Library* built A.D. 110–120. The two-storey façade is now restored. Behind was a single lofty three-storeyed hall with galleries for access to the cupboards in which the books (in manuscript form) were stored. Outer walling, separated from the hall wall by an ambulatory corridor, ensured that no dampness could seep inside.

Extensive Roman civic remains have been excavated in other cities in this area, at *Pergamon*, *Miletos*, *Side*, *Sardis* and *Perge*. The colonnaded street, so characteristic of Asia Minor, is to be seen in most town layouts, in addition to the colonnaded stoas which surround the market place.

Domestic building has, in most towns, yet to be fully excavated. An exception is the site at Ephesos leading up the hillside off Curetes Street where two *insulae* and a number of private houses (*domus*) have been uncovered. The remains are extensive and in good condition showing frescoes, mosaics and marbles.

A most unusual design of *aqueduct* is the one built at *Aspendos*. Here, instead of the normal Roman practice of providing a gradual fall of the water channel—Vitruvius stated that a fall of 6 inches for every 100 feet was considered desirable—the water was carried under pressure across the broad valley. Two pressure towers (PLATE 40) were constructed to divide the long aqueduct into three parts. Since the water had to be raised to the top of the acropolis over a distance of a kilometre, this saved the construction of an aqueduct 100 feet high over this long distance.

THE EARLY CHRISTIAN CHURCH

There was no Christian architecture before A.D. 200; believers gathered together to meet in each others' homes and used the courtyard fountain for baptism. During the third century Christians became far more numerous, including important citizens in their numbers. This led to a period of persecution when large gatherings were prohibited, but by A.D. 260 the authorities tolerated—if

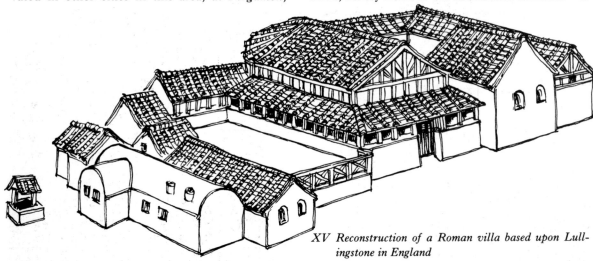

XV *Reconstruction of a Roman villa based upon Lull-ingstone in England*

Plate 39   Hellenistic Gate, Perge, Turkey, second century A.D. Adapted into a nymphaeum *c.* 120 A.D.

Plate 40   The aqueduct, Aspendos, Turkey, second century A.D. One of the pressure towers

not legalized—Christian activities, and purpose-built structures began to be erected. These buildings were simple, their style based up classical domestic architecture (pages 75–82 and **III, IV** and **XV**). They were Christian community houses which contained rooms for (among other purposes) meals, for meeting and for services, for funerals, baptism and confirmation.

In A.D. 313 the Roman Emperor Constantine issued the Edict of Milan which gave to Christians the legal right to practise their religion openly on an equal basis with other religions and, after A.D. 325, Christianity became the official religion of the empire. From this time onward Christian churches were built for the purpose of worship and a form of Christian architecture developed. Until his death in A.D. 337, many of the more important churches were inaugurated by Constantine himself: S. Peter's Basilica in Rome was the greatest of these, built to house the shrine of the Apostle Peter. The basilica, completed in A.D. 329, was 391 feet long and 208 feet wide. Standing in the huge apse, covered by a *baldacchino*, was the monument to Peter. The adjacent transept (an unusual feature at this time) accommodated the crowds who came to pay homage to the memoria of the apostle enshrined there. This basilica was replaced during the Renaissance by that now standing up on the site (Volume 2).

When the form of the Christian church was being developed, it was clear that a different type of design was required from that of the classical temple (pages 56–63), which had evolved to house

not the worshippers, but a representation of the deity. Christians needed a building which would be dignified yet practical. It had to contain a sanctuary for the clergy, where Mass would be said, a lay part for the congregation (the nave), a forecourt (atrium) where postulants and unbelievers could assemble and, in later instances, a martyrium to shelter the relics of graves of the martyr to whom the church was dedicated (**XVI**).

The form of structure chosen was that of the Roman basilica (pages 55–6 and **XII**), and, from this, evolved the Christian basilican church. In the time of Constantine there was no standard design of basilica; variations were incorporated according to local needs and wishes. Some large examples in important towns such as Rome, Constantinople, Milan, Trier and in the Holy Land were complex designs (pages 94, 96 and **173** and **XVII**) which might possess more than one hall, or were multi-aisled and had several apses. Others were simple and unpretentious.

Early Christian churches were of brick and concrete, some in stone, and were plain on the exterior. Inside was glowing colour, the ornamen-

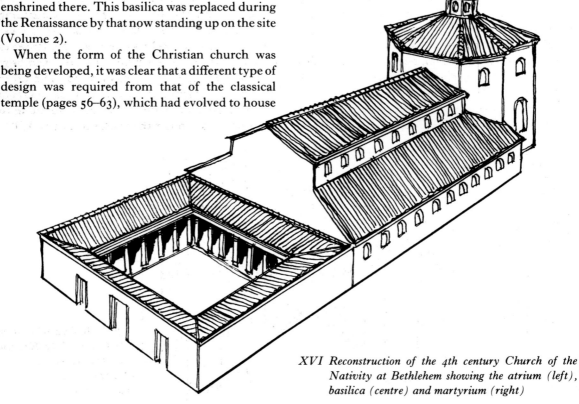

XVI Reconstruction of the 4th century Church of the Nativity at Bethlehem showing the atrium (left), basilica (centre) and martyrium (right)

tation in coloured marbles, mosaic, painting and gilding. Before the end of the fifth century there was no specific alignment of the church to face the east with the altar placed at the east end. Indeed, many early basilicas built before this are still aligned towards the west, S. Peter's in Rome, for example. There were no bell towers; these were added later.

XVII Reconstruction of the Emperor Constantine's Lateran Basilica in Rome. The Basilica Constanina, now the Cathedral of Rome, S. Giovanni in Laterano, has since been many times altered and added to

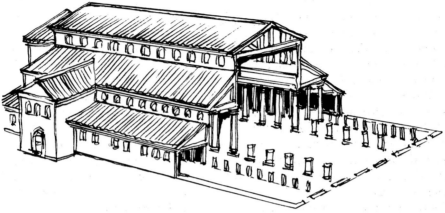

Istanbul

As described on page 104, not a great deal survives of the great capital city of the eastern half of the later Roman Empire. What does still exist—apart from the ecclesiastical Byzantine heritage, notably the great church of S. Sophia (pages 104–6), are major military and engineering structures so typical of all Roman cities. Considerable remains survive of the great *city walls* begun by Theodosius in A.D. 413 and, particularly notable is the fourth century *aqueduct* built under the Emperor Valens which was about 3500 feet long; about three quarters of this remains. Also, most impressive,

are the *cisterns* of Istanbul. Two of the great covered cisterns exist. These are great vaulted underground caverns, the roof supported by columns which display a wide variety of capital design. The larger example is the sixth century *Yerebatan Sarayi*. It was a reservoir containing water for the palaces of the city, water which was brought from the Belgrade Forest 19 kilometres distant. 336 columns support the brick vaulting; they are arranged in 12 rows of 28. The other cistern, the *Binbirdirek* (Cistern of 1001 columns) is also of the sixth century. It has 224 columns in 16 rows of 14 to support the brick vaulting (**XVIII**).

XVIII Binbirdirek Cistern (the Cistern of the Thousand-and-One Columns), Constantinople, sixth century

Glossary

The reference figures in brackets refer to illustrations in
the text.

Abacus The top member of a capital, usually a square or curved-sided slab of stone or marble (**plate 4**).

Abutment The solid mass of masonry or brickwork from which an arch springs, or against which it abuts.

Acanthus A leaf form used in classical ornament.

Acropolis A city upon a hill, a citadel. A Greek term usually also implying some fortification (**29**).

Acroteria Blocks resting upon the vertex and lower extremities of a pediment to carry carved ornament (**34**).

Adytum In temple architecture, an inner sanctuary.

Aeolic capital A primitive palmette type of Ionic capital evolved by the Greeks in Asia Minor (**28**).

Agora A Greek word for the open-air meeting place to be found in Greek city centres which was used for the transaction of business and which included a market-place, shops, business premises and stoas (**I**).

Ala An outer passage round the side walls of an Etruscan temple (**VI**).

Anta A pilaster built against the wall on either side of a temple portico. When the portico has columns between such antae so that they range with the front wall, the portico is described as being *in antis*. Thus, a *distyle in antis* temple has two columns between the antae.

Antefixae Carved blocks set at regular intervals along the lower edge of a roof in classical architecture (**42**).

Anthemion A type of classical ornament based upon the honeysuckle flower (**62**).

Apse Semicircular or polygonal termination to an elevation of a basilica or church (**240**).

Arabesque Classical ornament in delicate, flowing forms, terminating in scrolls and decorated with flowers and leaves (**105**).

Architrave The lowest member of the classical entablature (**23**)

Arcuated construction Where the structure is supported on arches (**121**).

Arris The vertical sharp edges between flutes on a column or pilaster (**23**).

Arcuated lintel A term describing an entablature which is in part arched-up. Of Syrian origin and may be referred to as a 'Syrian arch' (**133**).

Articulation The designing, defining and dividing up of a façade into vertical and horizontal architectural members.

Ashlar Hewn and squared stones prepared for building and laid in horizontal courses.

Atrium In domestic ancient classical architecture a central hall or open courtyard surrounded by rooms. In the centre of the roof was an open part called the *compluvium*. Rainwater ran from the eaves, through the gutters and fed a cistern or fountain basin below: this was termed the *impluvium* (**III, 144, 145**). In Early Christian and Byzantine churches a colonnaded entrance forecourt.

Baldacchino A canopy supported on pillars over an altar or throne.

Barrel vault A continuous vault in semicircular section like a tunnel (**125A**).

Basilica In Roman architecture a hall of justice and centre for commercial exchange. In Imperial Rome large basilicas were roofed by coffered vaults of brick and concrete supported on massive piers. The hall was rectangular in ground plan with an apse at one end (**110A**). The basilican form was adapted by the early Christians for their churches. In these, columns divided the nave from the aisles and these supported a wooden open roof. The basilican plan continued in use for several centuries (**173**).

Bema In Ancient Athens a raised platform in a place of public assembly. Adapted later in Early Christian church design as a raised stage, generally at the apsidal end of a basilica, for the use of the clergy.

Bouleuterion Greek city council house (**I, II**).

Bucranium A classical decorative motif representing the frontal view of an ox skull. Used especially in the metopes of a Doric frieze.

Caementa An aggregate made up of lumps of stone or brick used in Roman concrete.

Caldarium A hot room in a Roman Baths.

Capital The crowning feature of a column or pier (**176** and **plate 21**).

Caryatid Sculptured female figure in the form of a support or column (**plate 11**).

Cavea The auditorium of a classical theatre. The name derives from the design of Greek theatre which was cut out from a hillside (**57**). The word is also applied to the seating in an amphitheatre (**129**).

Cella The main chamber or sanctuary in a Roman temple which houses the cult image (**112, 113**).

Cenaculum Dining room in a Roman house.

Centering A structure, usually made of wood, set up to support a dome, vault or arch until construction is complete (**IX**).

Coffer A panel or caisson sunk into a ceiling, vault or dome. Most commonly the coffer is octagonal in shape and decoratively carved (**108**).

Conch The domed ceiling of a semicircular apse (**plate 31**).

Console A decorative scrolled bracket used in classical architecture to support a cornice. A *modillion* is similar but most often consoles are taller than they are wide and are used in doorway design, each flanking the door frame (**139**), while modillions are wider than high and support a deeply projecting length of cornice (**167**).

Corbel A projecting block of stone, brick or wood, often decoratively carved, which acts as a support.

Cornice The crowning member of a classical entablature (**23**).

Crepidoma The stepped base of a Greek temple (**50**).

Crossing The central area in a cruciform church where the transepts cross the nave and choir arm. In Byzantine architecture this space is often covered by a dome and drum (**208, 209**).

Cruciform A plan based on the form of a cross.

Cryptoportico An underground vaulted passage often lit obliquely through the vault.

Cubicula Sleeping apartments in a Roman house.

Cuneus In a theatre or amphitheatre the wedge-shaped blocks of seating (**56**).

Curia The assembly building of the Roman Senate (**85**).

Cyclopean masonry Walling consisting of immense blocks of stone as seen in building at Tyrins and Mycenae. Named after the mythical Cyclopes (**9**).

Decastyle Comprising ten columns.

Dentil A form of classical ornament comprising a row of small rectangular blocks (**26**).

Dipteral Describes a peristyle composed of a double row of columns.

Domical vault A dome-shaped vault where the ribs or groins are semicircular in shape so causing the centre of the vaulted bay to rise higher than the side arches.

Domus A Roman town house.

Dosseret A deep block often placed above the Byzantine capital to support the wide voussoirs of the arch above (**plate 30**).

Dromos A sloping or horizontal passage serving as the entrance to an underground chamber-tomb (**12**).

Drum The circular or poly-sided walling, usually pierced with windows, supporting a dome (**181**).

Echinos A curved moulded member supporting the abacus of the Doric Order. The term is derived from the Greek *echinos*, meaning sea urchin. The curve resembles the shell of the sea urchin (**plate 4**).

Entablature The continuous horizontal lintel made up of mouldings and supported by columns characteristic of classical architecture (**90, 91, 95**).

Entasis Taken from the Greek word for distension, is a convex curving along the outline of a column shaft. It is designed to correct the optical illusion which gives to a shaft bounded by straight lines the appearance of being concave.

Epinaos The open space under the portico roof at the rear of a classical temple behind the naos.

Exedra A small room, niche or recess in a classical building.

Extrados The outer curved face of an arch or vault.

Fastigium Roof, gable or pediment

Fillet A narrow flat band which divides mouldings from one another, also separates column flutes (**94**).

Flute Vertical channelling in the shaft of a column (**17**).

Forum The Roman place of assembly for markets, temples, court of justice, etc. (**85**).

Frieze In classical architecture the central section of the entablature (**23**).

Frigidarium The cold water swimming bath in a Roman Baths.

Greek cross plan A cruciform plan where the four arms of the cross are of equal length (**209**).

Groined vault One covering a square bay where two barrel vaults, of equal diameter and height, intersect.

Guilloche Classical ornament in the form of an intertwined plait.

Guttae Small cones under the mutules and triglyphs of the Doric entablature (**23**).

Gymnasium A Greek centre for sport and culture which would include an exercise room, a running track, bathing and changing facilities and lecture, study and library facilities.

Hellenistic The time of later Greek culture between the age of Alexander and the Roman takeover (*c.* 320–146 B.C.).

Hippodromos A long track with curved end (or ends) used for horse and chariot racing. Equivalent of the Roman *circus* and to be found in many cities.

Hypocaust An underfloor chamber of brick or stone constructed in Ancient Roman buildings for central heating purposes. Hot air in the basement furnace passed under the floor and through flues to heat the walls in all rooms (**XI**)

Iconostasis In a Byzantine church the screen wall covered with icons which separates nave from chancel.

Imbrex (pl. *imbrices*) A Roman rounded tile used in roofing to cover the joints between the flat tiles (*tegulae*).

Impost The upper course of a wall from where an arch or vault springs. An *impost block* marks this part of the wall.

Insula Roman multi-storey tenement block (**151**).

Intercolumniation The space between columns (**34**).

Intersecting vault Where two vaults, either of semi-circular or pointed form, meet at right angles (**140**).

Kokoshniki Term used in Russia for the series of arches set in rows, generally in Byzantine construction. Derived from *Kokoshnik*, the name for a traditional headdress worn by Russian women and which the series of arches are thought to resemble (**246**).

Lintel The horizontal stone slab or timber beam spanning an opening and supported on columns or walls (**10**).

Martyrium A structure in an Early Christian church erected over the grave of a martyr or relics of such a martyr.

Megaron The chief apartment of a Mycenaean palace and of a Greek house (**8**).

Metope The space between the triglyphs of a Doric frieze. Often ornamented with carved sculpture (**plate 2**).

Modillion *See* Console.

Module A unit of measurement based on proportion by which parts of a classical order are regulated; the column shaft diameter (or half diameter) was so used.

Monolithic column One whose shaft is of one piece of stone, wood or marble in contrast to one made up from hollow drums.

Monopteral Describes a temple the roof of which is supported by columns but without walls.

Mutule Block attached under Doric cornices from which the guttae depend (**23**).

Naos In a Greek temple the sanctuary chamber containing the cult statue (**48**). In a Byzantine church, the sanctuary.

Narthex In an Early Christian or Byzantine church a vestibule extended transversely across the western end of the building, separated from the nave by a screen or wall and set apart as an area for women and penitents. Also known as an **antenave** or **antechurch** and, later, as a **galilee** (**196, 242**).

Odeion A Greek roofed theatre used generally for concerts or lectures.

Opisthodomus An enclosed area at the rear of the naos in a Greek temple, often utilised as a treasury.

Orchestra The circular area in a Greek theatre where the chorus danced and sang (**56**).

Palaestra Exercise area in a Greek gymnasium or Roman Baths.

Parakklesion In a Byzantine church, a chapel flanking the building or the narthex.

Pediment In classical architecture, the triangular low-pitched gable above the entablature which completes the end of the sloping roof (**34**).

Pendentive Spherical triangle formed by the intersecting of a dome by two pairs of opposite arches, themselves carried on piers or columns (**175, 190**).

Peripteral A building surrounded by columns (**111**).

Peristyle A row of columns surrounding a temple or court, also the space so enclosed (**141, 144**).

Pilaster A column of rectangular section engaged in the wall (**133**).

Podium A continuous projecting base or pedestal (**136**).

Pronaos In a temple, the area enclosed by side walls in front of the naos and behind the portico (**48**).

Propylon An important entrance gateway in Greek architecture as, for example, the entrance to the Athenian acropolis (**29**).

Proscenium The stage of a Hellenistic or Roman theatre (**XIV**).

Prostyle In temple design where the portico columns stand in front of the pronaos (**36**).

Pseudo-dipteral A temple where the peristyle is a double row of columns except for the part immediately surrounding the naos walls where there is only a single row.

Pseudo-peripteral A temple where the lateral columns are engaged with the cella wall; characteristic of Roman temples (**113**).

Pteroma The passageway or ambulatory between the naos walls of a Greek temple and the peristyle (**35**).

Pulpitum The raised platform of the stage of a Roman theatre.

Relieving arch An arch built into masonry walling to distribute the load and so prevent the weight above from crushing a lintel stone above an opening.

Rotunda A building of circular ground plan often surmounted by a dome. A circular apartment (**171, 172**).

Scaena (Greek **Skene**) Stage building of a Roman theatre (**125, 128**).

Shaft The column of an order between capital and base (**14, 15**).

Squinch Arches built diagonally across the internal corners of a square apartment and corbelled out to provide an octagonal base to support an octagonal or circular roofing (**V, 175**).

Stadion A Greek running track one stade (*c.* 600 feet) in length (**58**).

Stoa A Greek colonnaded structure, one- or two-storeyed, with an open front and shops or offices built into the rear wall (**38**).

Stylobate The platform upon which the columns of a Greek temple stand (**44**).

Tabularium A Roman structure to contain archives.

Tegula A Roman roof tile.

Temenos The sacred precinct surrounding or adjacent to a temple.

Tepidarium Room of moderate heat in a Roman Baths (**150**).

Thermae Under the Roman Empire a bathing establishment for public or private use (**XIII**).

Tholos A circular temple, tomb or other building of this form (**plate 7**).

Trabeation A type of construction using beams or lintels rather than arches.

Transept The arms of a cruciform church set at right angles to the nave and choir. Transepts are generally aligned north and south.

Travertine A calcareous building stone quarried near Tivoli and widely used in Roman building.

Triclinium A Roman dining room, so-called because of the arrangement of the reclining couches set on three sides of the apartment.

Triglyph The blocks cut with vertical channels set at intervals along the frieze of the Greek Doric Order (**23**).

Tufa A lightweight sponge-like limestone formed by water precipitating a lime deposit from older adjacent limestone. The many varieties of this stone were quarried in Latium and Campania and were widely used in the days of ancient Rome especially for vaulting because of the lightweight quality of the material.

Tympanum The face of a classical pediment between its sloping and horizontal cornice mouldings. Tympana are generally carved and/or sculptured (**34**).

Velarium An awning set up to provide shade over a theatre or amphitheatre.

Volute A spiral or scroll to be seen in Ionic, Corinthian and Composite capitals (**plates 5** and **20**).

Vomitorium Entrance to the *cavea* of a theatre or amphitheatre.

Voussoir The wedge-shaped blocks which comprise an arch (**71**).

Bibliography

A classified list of books recommended for further reading.

General

ALLSOPP, B., *A History of Classical Architecture*, Pitman, 1965

CHITHAM, R., *The Classical Orders of Architecture*, Architectural Press, 1985

COPPLESTONE, T., Ed., *World Architecture*, Hamlyn, 1963

FLETCHER, BANISTER, *A History of Architecture*, Butterworth, 1987

JORDAN, R. FURNEAUX, *European Architecture in Colour*, Thames and Hudson, 1961; *A Concise History of Western Architecture*, Thames and Hudson, 1969

KOSTOF, S., *A History of Architecture*, Oxford University Press, 1985

NORWICH, J. J. Ed., *Great Architecture of the World*, Mitchell Beazley, 1975.

NUTTGENS, P., *The Story of Architecture*, Phaidon Press, 1983; *The World's Great Architecture*, Hamlyn, 1980

PEVSNER, N., *An Outline of European Architecture*, Penguin Books, 1961

RAEBURN, M., Ed., *Architecture of the Western World*, Orbis Publishing, 1980; *An Outline of World Architecture*, Octopus 1973

TRACHTENBERG, M., and HYMAN, I., *Architecture: From Prehistory to Post-Modernism*, Academy Editions, 1986

WATKIN, D., *A History of Western Architecture*, Barrie and Jenkins, 1986

YARWOOD, D., *The Architecture of Italy*, Chatto and Windus, 1970; *A Chronology of Western Architecture*, Batsford, 1987

Greek

AKURGAL, E., *Ancient Civilisations and Ruins of Turkey*, Haşet Kitabevi, Istanbul, 1973

ASHMOLE, B., *Architect and Sculptor in Classical Greece*, Phaidon, 1972

DINSMOOR, W. B., *The Architecture of Ancient Greece*, Batsford, 1950

LAWRENCE, A. W., *Greek Architecture*, Pelican History of Art Series, Penguin, 1983

PLOMMER, H., *Ancient and Classical Architecture*, Longmans, Green, 1959

RICHTER, G. M. A., *Greek Art*, Phaidon, 1959

ROBERTSON, D. S., *Greek and Roman Architecture*, Cambridge University Press, 1969

SCRANTON, R. L., *Greek Architecture*, Prentice-Hall International, 1979

TAYLOR, W., *Greek Architecture*, Arthur Barker, 1971

Etruscan and Roman

BOETHIUS, A., *Etruscan and Early Roman Architecture*, Pelican History of Art Series, Penguin, 1978

BRION, M., and SMITH, E., *Pompeii and Herculaneum*, Elek, 1960

HODGE, P., *The Roman House*, Longman, 1977

MACDONALD, W. L., *The Architecture of the Roman Empire*, Yale University Press, 1965

PICARD, G., *Roman Architecture*, Oldbourne, 1965

PLOMMER, H., *Ancient and Classical Architecture*, Longmans, Green, 1959

ROBERTSON, D. S., *Greek and Roman Architecture*, Cambridge University Press, 1969

SEAR, F., *Roman Architecture*, Batsford, 1982

VIGHI, R., *Villa Hadriana*, Nardini, Rome

WARD-PERKINS, J. B., *Roman Architecture*, Abrams, New York, 1978; *Roman Imperial Architecture*, Pelican History of Art Series, Penguin, 1981

WHEELER, M., *Roman Art and Architecture*, Thames and Hudson, 1964

Early Christian and Byzantine

HODDINOTT, R. F., *Early Byzantine Churches in Macedonia and Southern Serbia*, Macmillan, 1963

KÄHLER, H., and MANGO, C., *Hagia Sophia*, Zwemmer, 1967

KRAUTHEIMER, R., *Early Christian and Byzantine Architecture*, Pelican History of Art Series, Penguin, 1981

MANGO, C., *Byzantine Architecture*, Faber and Faber, 1978

STEWART, C., *Byzantine Legacy*, Allen and Unwin, 1959; *Early Christian, Byzantine and Romanesque Architecture*, Longmans Green, 1959; *Serbian Legacy*, Allen and Unwin, 1959

TALBOT RICE, D., *Art of the Byzantine Era*, Thames and Hudson, 1963; *Constantinople*, Elek, 1965

Index